Chris Foxon and D.E.M. Productions
in association with Belka Productions present

The West End premiere of

DONKEY HEART

by Moses Raine

First performed at the Old Red Lion Theatre, London,
on Tuesday, 6 May 2014

First performed at Trafalgar Studios, London,
on Wednesday, 7 January 2015

DONKEY HEART
by Moses Raine

Cast
in order of speaking:

Patrick Godfrey	**Alexander**
Lisa Diveney	**Sasha**
Paul Wyett	**Ivan**
Alex Large	**Thomas**
Pierre Atri/Albie Marber	**Kolya**
Georgia Henshaw	**Clara**
James Musgrave	**Petya**
Amanda Root	**Zhenya**
Emily Bruni	**Natalia**

Creative Team

Nina Raine	**Director**
James Turner	**Designer**
Peter Mumford	**Lighting Designer**
Alex Caplen	**Sound Designer**
Chris Foxon	**Lead Producer**
Ramin Sabi	**Producer**
Oliver King	**Associate Producer**
Miguel Vicente	**Associate Lighting Designer**
Emily Jones	**Casting Director**
Tamsin Rose/James Ashby	**Production Managers**
Holly Rose Henshaw	**Costume Supervisor**
Roisin Symes	**Stage Manager**
Jonny Kelly	**Assistant Director**
Anna Driftmier	**Design Assistant**

The action takes place in Moscow in the present day.

The performance lasts approximately two hours and fifteen minutes including an interval of fifteen minutes.

Donkey Heart was first produced by Chris Foxon at the Old Red Lion Theatre, London, in May 2014. This production features the original cast and creative team with the exception of the role of Zhenya, which was performed by Wendy Nottingham at the Old Red Lion Theatre and by Amanda Root at Trafalgar Studios.

Production Acknowledgements

Press Representative | **Sue Hyman Associates Ltd**
www.suehyman.com
Graphic Design | **Rebecca Pitt**
Production Photography | **Robert Workman**
Rehearsal Spaces | **St Gabriel's Halls** and **Pushkin House**

The producers would like to thank:
Apiary Studios, Amy Ball, Chats Palace, Holly Gladwell, Simon Godwin, Hampstead Theatre, Lotte Hines, IdeasTap, Hannah Jenner, Lisa Makin, Patrick and Debra Marber, Anne McNulty, Lydia Slater, Julia Rochester, Kate Brayn, Richard Lee, Svetlana Adjoubei & Academia Rossica, Karina Baldry & Russian Revels, Ksenia Bobkova, Theodora Clarke, Andrei Fomin & everyone at Banya No 1, Mariana Haseldine, Anna Kornilova, William MacDougall, Alexandra May, Oleg Mirochnikov, Anna Nuzhnaya, Russians in the UK, Hamid Sabi, Ursula Woolley & everyone at Pushkin House, Jan Woroniecki and Mascha Zherebtsova.

Donkey Heart

Moses Raine was shortlisted for the Verity Bargate Award for his first play, *The Survival Handbook*. His next play, *Shrieks of Laughter*, was staged at the Soho Theatre. He has co-written the finale to the hit television series *Mistresses* and is currently adapting a short story by Ian McEwan for film.

also by Moses Raine from Faber

SHRIEKS OF LAUGHTER

MOSES RAINE

Donkey Heart

FABER & FABER

First published in 2014
by Faber and Faber Limited
74–77 Great Russell Street, London WC1B 3DA

Typeset by Country Setting, Kingsdown, Kent CT14 8ES
Printed in England by CPI Group (UK) Ltd, Croydon CR0 4YY

All rights reserved
© Moses Raine, 2014

The right of Moses Raine to be identified as author
of this work has been asserted in accordance with Section 77
of the Copyright, Designs and Patents Act 1988

All rights whatsoever in this work are strictly reserved.
Applications for permission for any use whatsoever including
performance rights must be made in advance, prior to any such
proposed use, to Casarotto Ramsay and Associates Ltd,
Waverley House, 7–12 Noel Street, London W1F 8GQ
(email: rights@casarotto.co.uk). No performance
may be given unless a licence has first been obtained

*This book is sold subject to the condition that it shall not,
by way of trade or otherwise, be lent, resold, hired out or
otherwise circulated without the publisher's prior consent
in any form of binding or cover other than that in which
it is published and without a similar condition including
this condition being imposed on the subsequent purchaser*

A CIP record for this book is available from the British Library

ISBN 978–0–571–31783–7

2 4 6 8 10 9 7 5 3

For My Mother

May the winds welcome you with softness.
May the sun bless you with his warm hands.
May you fly so high and so well that God
   joins you in laughter,
And sets you gently back into the loving arms
   of Mother Earth.

With all my love, Momo
x

Acknowledgements

Friends, mentors, godparents . . .
I would like to thank you from the bottom of my heart.

Julian Barnes and Pat Kavanagh, Chris Foxon, Oliver Rowse, Christopher Reid, Ian McEwan and Annalena McAfee, William Boyd and Susan Boyd, James Fenton and Darryl Pinkney, Tatiana Andersen Camre, Francis Wyndham, Alan Hollinghurst, Larissa Haskell, Piers Wenger, Damien Timmer, Rebecca Keane, Alan Bennett, Tom Stoppard, Bella Freud and James Fox, Dinah Wood, Steve King, Fred Sugarman-Warner, Joe Charlton, Nick Hudson, Patrick Hunter, John Bails, Rachel Taylor, Mel Kenyon, Evgeny Pasternak, Lily Barwise, Nana and Grandpa.

I am indebted to my father, and my sister, Nina.
Thank you for giving me the guts to carry on.
I would be nothing without my two brothers –
who always give me the best material.

I'd also like to thank the fantastic Christina Rogers.

Characters

Alexander
the grandfather

Ivan
Alexander's son, married to Zhenya

Zhenya
Ivan's wife
She has a nervous tic of sniffing all the time

Sasha
their daughter, twenty-four years old

Petya
their son, eighteen years old

Kolya
their son, ten years old

Clara
Petya's girlfriend, eighteen years old

Thomas
an English guest, mid-twenties

Natalia
a friend and employee, late twenties

The play is set in a flat in central Moscow in the present day. All the action takes place in one room – the overcrowded sitting room. There is a door stage left exiting to the front door. Stage right there is a door leading to the bedrooms and a small kitchen.

Note on the Dialogue

When the Russian characters speak English to Thomas it is spoken with a Russian accent. When the Russian characters talk among themselves they speak English with no accent.

Act One

SCENE ONE

Early morning. A darkened sitting room. Petya sleeps on the sofa, fully dressed.
   Alexander enters. The old man shuffles, a glum expression on his face. His moth-eaten suit jacket covers flannel pyjamas. He is wearing a necklace with a passport-sized photo attached. He kisses the photograph and says to it . . .

Alexander Good morning, Kolya.

He turns on a lamp, and sees Petya asleep. He shakes his head and sighs.
   He goes to a rope and lets down a hanging dryer. He takes his trousers from the dryer and smells them. They are still damp. He lays them on a small table. Armed with a pink hairdryer he dries the trousers.
   A moment passes. Sasha enters. She's sleepy in a dressing gown.

Sasha Priviet.

Sasha looks at her watch and then at Alexander drying his trousers.

Alexander Sasha, you look tired, go back to bed.

Sasha Can't sleep . . .

Alexander Well, I had awful indigestion all night long.

Beat.

Sasha Couldn't you do that later?

Alexander nods 'yes' but continues. Sasha sniffs the air.

Sasha Drains?

Alexander Fish heads for lunch. Your mother wanted to throw them away.

Ivan enters. He kisses his daughter good morning.

Ivan Christ, Pa, it stinks – what're you cooking? Smells like a whore's thong out there.

Sasha Fish heads. Mama threw them away.

Alexander In the bin! I'll make a beautiful fish soup.

Ivan Oh yeah – cream of gusset.

Alexander looks haughty. Thomas enters, bleary eyed. Alexander stands up and shakes hands with him.

Alexander Our guest! Welcome!

Sasha/Ivan Priviet.

Thomas Hi, I mean private –

Sasha It's 'Priviet'.

Thomas 'Priviet'? Priviet, Alexandervich –

Sasha (*smiling*) Alexander Maximovich.

Everyone nods 'hello' to him and smiles widely.

Alexander Does Thomas want something for breakfast?

Sasha What'd you like to eat?

Thomas Oh, I'm fine thanks – quick smoke, that's all.

Alexander (*to Sasha*) He can have bread and jam.

Thomas (*to Sasha*) Someone warned me about Russian breakfasts.
Apparently you lot eat butter in your porridge?

Sasha It's true. (*To Alexander.*) He says he's fine.

Ivan He's holding out for fish heads, Dad.

Thomas grasps Alexander's arm and grins wildly.

Thomas I'll have something, Alexander Maximovich – was that right? You choose, tell him to choose for me, Sasha.

Sasha (*to Alexander*) He says he'll have something, you choose.

Alexander exits. Ivan covertly observes Sasha and Thomas. Sasha lifts up the hairdryer.

Thomas Why the hairdryer?

Sasha The state. No heating till October.

Thomas What if it's cold?

Sasha Wear another pair of earrings, darling.

Sasha turns the hairdryer on and continues with her grandfather's job. Thomas looks at Petya asleep on the sofa.

Sasha He's fine.

Ivan (*wild grin*) Drenk.

Thomas doesn't understand. Sasha turns the hairdryer off.

Sasha Drunk . . . always the same, him and his girlfriend. They go out and come back drunk with big dreams, 'We're moving to Paris! Clara's going to be a waitress, I'm going to teach a piano.' And everyone says, 'Petya, Paris is great city.'

Thomas It is –

Sasha Nah, Paris is okay . . . it's provincial. When the next night comes, 'Munich! We're moving to Munich.' And everyone goes, 'Oh when, Petya, when?' Never! That's when! He never bloody goes!

Thomas laughs, Sasha shakes her head.

Their talking, didn't keep you up?

Thomas Oh not at all. I did hear shouting at one point.

Sasha Friendly shouting, I promise. I tell them be quieter.

Thomas God don't, I felt bad enough gypping his bed.

Ivan stands up and retreats to the toilet. Thomas and Sasha are alone. He walks to her and sits on the side of her armchair. There is a different atmosphere – suddenly.

Sasha And so far, mm, tell me tell me –

Thomas Petya picked me up at the airport.

Sasha I know.

Thomas He insisted on driving all the way back on the hard shoulder?

Sasha (*smiling*) That's normal.

Thomas It's retarded.

Thomas looks round the room.

And I mean the roads aren't great, are they?
Full of potholes. Lots of birch trees.

Sasha I like our countryside.

Thomas Oh it's epic, epic . . .

Thomas brushes Sasha's face with a finger. She looks up at him – they look into each other's eyes. He wants to kiss her but something is stopping him.

Sasha Mm, what else, what else –

Thomas stands up.

Thomas Oh well, when we flew in. Huge forests as far as . . .

The sky does go on forever here . . . it's vast.

Thomas is drawn back to Sasha. He strokes her face. She smiles.

Sasha What're you doing?

Thomas I think I'm happy to see you.

They look intently at each other.

Sasha Thank you for coming.

A door slams from off and they part in a panic. Kolya shoots through the room on his scooter.

Kolya Priviet! Wo-woo! Priviet!

Sasha This is Kolya.

But Kolya has gone. Sasha calls after him.

Kolya! Kolya! Come and say hello to my guest.

Kolya enters, shyly.

Kolya, this is Thomas, do you remember me saying . . .

Thomas Kak dela, moi malenki? Harasho?

Kolya nods blankly. In a hoarse whisper, eyes always on Thomas, he says to Sasha with real pity:

Kolya Has he had a stroke?

Thomas I'm Tom . . . What's 'I'm Tom'?

Sasha (*raised eyebrow*) Very complicate. Ya Tom.

A toilet flushes, offstage. Thomas puts his hand on his chest.

Thomas Ya Tom. Priviet.

Ivan enters, drying his hands and pats Kolya's head.

Ivan Kolya – have you got your rucksack ready?

Kolya Yes, Papa.

Ivan (*to Sasha in an undertone, re Tom*) How long's he staying?

Sasha I know, I'll sort it out.

Alexander enters with a steaming bowl of porridge.

Alexander Breakfast is served!

Alexander hands the bowl of porridge to Thomas. Kolya starts making a row like a steam train.

Kotik, what are you doing?

Kolya I'm a train.

Alexander I thought you were a duck.

Kolya Yesterday Dyedu, yesterday!

Alexander Yesterday he was a duck, today he is a train. Tomorrow he'll be a –

Kolya A blacksmith, people'll say, 'Blacksmith mend my horse,' and I'll say –

Alexander 'Sorry, today I'm a duck.'

Everyone laughs.

Kolya NO! *No*, I'll say –

Ivan Quack quack quack.

Kolya is desperate, they're all laughing at him.

Kolya I'll say, 'Beautiful horse, let's change your shoes – This *stupid old man* has put you in slippers.'

Sasha How's your breakfast?

Thomas (*sickly smile*) It's great.

Thomas forces the spoon to his withering mouth. Sasha looks in the bowl.

Sasha (*to Alexander*) You put butter in his porridge! (*To Thomas.*) I'm so sorry, you don't eat this –

Thomas NO! I want to!

He manfully shovels another huge spoonful into his already full mouth.

Sasha I'm throwing this away –

Alexander Don't waste food. He's lucky to be eating. Tell him I ate buttons, Sasha!

Sasha prises the porridge from Thomas and places it on the coffee table.

Kolya Chocolate ones?

Alexander I ate the buttons from my coat.

Ivan (*to Kolya*) He didn't –

Alexander I did! It's a true story –

Ivan He ate the stuff buttons were made of – a soft plastic –

Alexander In sheets. (*Brightly.*) We stole it. Yeah, we'd mould cutlets out of it. White buttons were sweeter than the brown ones.

He starts eating the discarded porridge.

Thomas (*to Sasha*) Is he offended?

Sasha In the war, he was stuck in Leningrad, the siege, y'know.
　He always never forgets . . . it's not your fault . . .
　We all had to queue for food, even in the late eighties. When I was a little girl, even. We all remember it.

Thomas You remember it?

Ivan watches his father. Alexander is holding a spoonful of porridge out for Kolya to eat. Kolya eats it and smiles.

Sasha Mm. Hands in the cold, that's all I could see. So high, so all I could see . . . purple hands, people stamping their feet like horses. Freezing cold – what do you remember from childhood?

Thomas Pac-Man . . . The Legend of Zelda? . . . A computer game?
You remember not having food? Seriously?

Alexander runs his index finger round the bowl to scrape the very last of the porridge out and hands the empty bowl to Ivan.

Sasha Sure, the phone would ring, the phone rings, it's your friends . . .
Telling you maybe – eggs? So you phone your other friends, and tell them, eggs, and they phone their friends and no one worries about the phone bill, because state pay, no food but free telephone . . .
Before long, queues round the block. You'd run out with your bag . . . It's not like this nowadays, we don't drop our world for an egg. We live with like, communist hangover. Dry our clothes with a hairdryer . . .

Fade.

Blackout.

SCENE TWO

Petya sits with his laptop. Clara enters, brushing her hair.

Clara Hello, tummy.

Clara brushes her hair over the keyboard. Petya ignores this. Clara pokes Petya in the tummy.

Petya (*murmuring*) Who's Igor Shnitkin?

But Clara is looking for her shoes. A moment, then she looks up at Petya.

Clara Y'know what – you're fucking boring.

Petya (*distracted*) Mm, very interesting . . .

Clara slumps on Petya, and looks over his shoulder at the laptop.

Clara (*inquisitive*) Why're you looking at my Facebook page?

Petya Just am . . . interested . . .

Clara That's your *dad*'s laptop, Petya.

Petya points at the screen.

Petya Who's he?

Clara No one, boring, an old ex.

Petya If he's boring why did you upload photos of him?

Clara (*running her hand through his hair*) You've got photos of your exes on Facebook . . . your hair's thinning.

Petya My hair's not thinning? My hair's *fine*.

Clara Fine hair – bald by thirty.

Petya walks to the mirror. He runs his hands through his hair.

Petya It's thick!

Clara Vanity in men's actually really unattractive.

Petya You said my hair was thinning.

Petya sits down at the laptop and clicks away. Clara walks to him and repeatedly pokes him in the tummy with her hairbrush. Petya tries to ignore her.

Clara Are you ignoring me cos you're jealous of Igor Shnitkin . . .

She pokes him again.

Tummy!

Petya You're the fucking lard-arse.

Clara stalks away in a huff.

Clara I can't believe you'd actually say that?! What's your fucking problem –

Petya (*weary*) I was joking. I was clearly joking.

They look at each other: could amends be made? But Petya can't help looking back at the laptop.

Clara Go on then! You touch it more than me.

Petya shakes his head and stands up, arms opened.

Petya Come here.

Clara I'm not a dog. You don't own me!
(*Sulky.*) Anyone else would've asked me to marry them by now.

Petya (*baffled*) Why?

Clara sulks. Petya playfully gets on one knee.

Clara . . . will you marry me?

Clara Fuck off, you need a proper job.

Petya laughs, stands up and hugs her. He gently gives her a love bite. Clara jumps away as if he's mortally wounded her.

Clara What's your problem? That actually really hurt, Petya.

Petya Oh really –

Clara Yes! It actually really hurt.
(*Looking in mirror.*) Oh m' God, you bruised me! You've bruised me – you actually bruised me . . . It's definitely a bruise.

Petya is annoyed. He goes to the laptop. Opens another window. Seems to read something that catches his attention. It's Clara's turn to make amends. She wheedles up to him, looks over his shoulder. Too late, Petya shields the laptop from her view, moves it.

Petya (*suddenly sour, losing it*) I'm trying to do some work!

She grabs the laptop off him.

Clara But you're not working!

She looks at the screen, double-takes, mystified.

Why are you looking at your dad's emails?

Petya snatches the laptop back off her.

Petya Fuck off!

Clara Why?

Petya Fuck off, that's why!

He reads intently off the laptop screen. Clara takes her hurt feelings for a sulk on the sofa. She is distracted by Thomas and Sasha, who enter with shopping. Clara stares inquisitively at Thomas. This is the first time she's seen the foreign guest. Petya is still absorbed with the laptop.

Sasha (*to Petya*) Mama's been banned from driving for two months.
She was driving the wrong way up a one-way street . . .

Petya (*distracted*) Oh God, not again. How much were they asking for?

Sasha Fifty, we didn't have it –

Petya Didn't she ask if she could pay later?

Sasha Yeah, but then he wanted to double the amount – that's Pa's laptop, Petya, you know he hates –

Petya (*snarl*) I know!!

He slaps it shut. They look at him, surprised.

Sasha Oh, also – you got another letter, Petya.

Sasha gives Petya the letter. He opens it, looks annoyed, and tosses it aside. Clara picks it up.

Clara This is from the army?!

Petya makes a face and a shrug.

But you said you'd sorted it out.

Petya I was busy.

Clara With what? With Facebook!

Petya Clara –

Clara No! Actually no!

Petya Ahh Jesus, please shut up –

Petya is packing his dad's laptop back in its case.

Clara When are you going to do something about it?

Petya It's fine, there'll be a doctor Mama can bribe.

Clara But you've had loads of those letters, and they'll come and actually arrest you if you don't sort it out. There'll be a knock at the door –

Sasha She's right, they can arrest you for skiving.

Petya And I'm going to sort it out, so can you please all fuck off.

Thomas (*to Sasha*) What's going on?

Sasha You know, National Service, it's compulsory thing if you aren't at college . . . Petya was kicked off his course for things we don't speak about, so very quickly he has many many letters telling he must to do his army.
   (*Kindly.*) Do you still need poops?

   Thomas starts laughing.

Thomas Yeah. God, that's embarrassing. Is it that obvious?

Sasha Well, you know where it is. Through there.

Thomas Yup.

   Thomas hurries offstage. Sasha goes to the mirror and looks at herself.

Clara I can see you, Sasha . . .

Sasha I can see you too, Clara.

   Sasha raises her eyebrows and shakes her head. She runs her hand through hair, turns head to the left with a vague pout. Clara laughs.

Clara You *so* fancy him.

Sasha (*ignoring Clara*) Petya – do I have dandruff?

   Petya sits next to Clara, but she is being distant with him.

Clara (*to Sasha*) Who is he?

Sasha No one, a friend I made in England. He's doing a language course here.

Clara Have you had sex?

Sasha Clara . . . please . . .

   Petya fondles Clara's knee but she ignores him.

Petya (*to Clara, baby voice*) Baby? Are you still sulking with me?

Clara I don't give a shit about you.

Petya I'm sorry . . . I'm sorry I got jealous about the photos. I'm sorry I was grumpy.

Petya pulls Clara into his arms.

Clara Thing about you, Petya. Your heart's in the right place . . .
So it's a real pity – your cock's on y'forehead.

Clara laughs at her joke. Petya takes the abuse. They kiss. The front door opens, Zhenya and Alexander enter, out of breath. Alexander immediately starts rummaging through a desk drawer.

Zhenya Petya – help, go –
Go and get the rest of the shopping.
(*To Alexander.*) Sit down –

Alexander I'm a little faint, that's all.

Zhenya Petya – please!

Alexander Have you seen them?

Sasha Seen what, Dedushka?

Zhenya Sit down –

Alexander But I don't want to sit down.

Zhenya Petya!

Sasha I'll get the shopping, Mama.

Zhenya plumps the cushions of Alexander's armchair. Sasha exits.

Zhenya Here you go, you sit down, I'll make a cup of tea.

Alexander ignores Zhenya and continues searching. Zhenya reads Petya's letter.

Alexander Pills, my pills, my heart pills –

Zhenya (*while reading letter, vague*) It's not your heart. You're heart's fine. It's the stairs, enough to kill anyone.

Alexander Why do I feel so faint? It's not normal. Do I look pale?

Petya It's your birthday, of course you look pale.

Zhenya (*holding letter up, worried*) Why haven't you sorted this out, Petya? You've got to sort this out.

Petya (*snarl*) Mama!

Clara I told him he needed to sort it out. Do you seriously want to end up in like Kosovo?! Is that like what you actually want –

Petya No one goes to Kosovo any more –

Clara You dunno, you actually could, y'know.

Zhenya We'll see Doctor Volkov about this, Petya.
  Masha's son Vasily saw him. You know Vasily –

Petya The nob.

Zhenya Masha paid two hundred dollars and Vasily only had to shave his eyebrows off.

Petya Well, that's a relief, only his eyebrows –

Clara (*delighted*) Ha ha, you're shaving your eyebrows off!

Petya No I'm not –

Zhenya You might have to . . .
  Doctor Volkov wrote a very nice letter for Vasily . . . Said he was mentally ill.

Alexander (*genuine*) What a nice man.

Petya (*more to himself*) I'm not shaving my eyebrows off.

Clara You probably would –

Petya I really wouldn't –

Clara In all fairness though, you probably would.

Petya No I wouldn't –

Clara But if it came to it –

Petya I'm not shaving my eyebrows off!

Clara (*sing-song*) Petya's shaving his eyebrows off.

Petya's had enough, he stalks out, slamming the door behind him.
  Clara is quick to follow, calling after him, 'Petya'.

Alexander (*to himself*) Young love, breaks hearts.

Something feels uncomfortable under Alexander's bottom. He digs about with his hands. He pulls out a container of pills.

(*Pleased.*) Ah. My heart pills . . .

He unscrews the cap and pours himself a handful and knocks them back.
  Kolya enters. He is playing with a burnt wine cork. He's drawn a toothbrush moustache on his face.

(*To Kolya.*) Have you done your homework? Shall I check it?

Kolya No, I'm Hitler.

Zhenya Let Dedushka check it, Kolya.

Kolya I'm busy, can't you see?!

Zhenya You're not busy, stop playing with the lighter . . .

Alexander Come and sit with me . . . Herr Führer.

Kolya sits by his grandfather and opens his exercise book.

Alexander Ah, maths . . . I hate maths. History's much more interesting.

I'll never forget my first history lesson at school. Our teacher asked, 'What's history?' And we didn't know what to say –

Kolya It's what happened before.

Alexander Yes, so she made us put our desks round the edge of the classroom and she stood up on a desk, this very fat woman. Very portly, and she walked all the way round the classroom, desk to desk – heaving great chest, and do you know what she said, Kolya? She said, 'You will never forget that. That's history.' I've never forgotten it . . . She couldn't spell either.

Where are your questions?

Kolya gives Alexander the worksheet.

Alexander (*reading*) 'If X amount of pineapple cost 7 each . . .'

We used to have questions about bags of kasha or beetroots . . .

Alexander reads the maths question. Ivan enters.

Ivan (*to Alexander*) Happy birthday.

Alexander Shh . . .

Alexander puts his reading glasses on his forehead. Ivan pours shot glasses of vodka out and hands them to family members.

Alexander (*mumble*) 'Pineapple cost 7 . . .' What have watermelon got to do with it? (*Panicked.*) My reading glasses, where are my glasses –

Kolya On your head . . . (*Hopeful.*) I think the answer's C.

Alexander But you're guessing, kotik.

Kolya No I'm not, that's the example question.

Alexander Is it?

Kolya The answer's there. 'Boria buys 4 pineapples . . .'

Alexander 'Boria buys 4 pineapples.' (*Deflated.*) I don't even like pineapple.

Ivan Here. Have a drink –

Ivan hands Alexander a vodka. Petya enters and sits on the sofa, texting on his phone. He looks very surly.
  Kolya looks into his grandfather's eyes, expectantly, waiting for the praise.
  Alexander strokes Kolya's head.

Kolya Well, say I'm cleverer than you!

Alexander You must be, kotik – you drew a moustache on your face.

Sasha stands in the doorway with shopping bags in each hand.

Zhenya (*to Sasha*) Oh, can you put it in the kitchen.

Ivan raises his glass and his eyebrows. This gets everyone's attention.

Ivan Shall we toast, choknim!

All Choknim!

They clink glasses.

Ivan How old are you, Pa?

Alexander X minus a hip?

Ivan (*smiling*) Happy birthday!

All Happy birthday!

They drink.

Ivan The best thing to follow a vodka . . . is another vodka.

Ivan clacks his tongue on his soft palate, and pours more vodkas. Meanwhile Zhenya violently spits on her apron and tries to wipe the moustache off Kolya's face. Petya is intent over his phone.

Zhenya Petya? Are you okay? . . . Where's Clara?

Petya (*dully*) Can you leave me alone?

Alexander (*to Ivan*) How was your day?

Ivan My P.A. left me in the lurch, her flatshare has fallen through. You know the one –

Zhenya (*overhearing this*) What's happened to Natalia? Is she okay, I still haven't answered her / email.

Ivan Hang about. (*To Alexander.*) My P.A., you know, lovely girl – dad died young, fifty. Collapsed in the doorway.

He taps his heart.

Kaput. Heart attack in the front room.

Alexander crosses himself, between the eyebrows.

(*To Zhenya.*) Her flatshare's fallen through, but I said she could stay with us –

Petya What! No way!

Ivan She's got nowhere to go, only a couple of days, till she finds her feet –

Petya No! People are always bloody coming! Like Sasha's dumb English friend –

Ivan Natalia's very nice, great arse –

Petya You don't even ask Mama, and you make an executive decision.

Zhenya It was only an idea, Petya –

Petya (*to Zhenya*) You already got her the job with Papa, just cos you done one thing doesn't mean you have to do more for / her.

Zhenya I was friends with her mother. Natalia was at the same school as Sasha.

Petya So?!

Zhenya She was very nice to Sasha when she was getting bullied.

Sasha I wasn't getting bullied –

Petya No. You were just a loner.

Alexander Mm, I'm interested in this heart attack, though.

Ivan Maybe it was a stroke, Pa, I can't remember.

Petya She can't stay with us. I don't want her here.
You wouldn't let Clara move in, when I wanted Clara –

Ivan Stop being a spoilt brat. (*Their eyes meet.*) And stop using my laptop.

Petya I haven't –

Zhenya Kolya, bathroom, now!

Kolya Nooo! I wanna look like Hitler –

Petya We're always having people / landed on us.

Kolya (*to Petya*) Draw a proper moustache on me.

Petya ignores Kolya's request, rails on.

Petya They come and stay and eat your food and you can't take a shit.

Ivan Jesus! If that's all you're het up about – there's a café on the corner.

Petya No! I want to shit here.

Ivan Then shit here! What's the problem!

Petya He's, in there, taking a shit –

Zhenya Keep your voice down –

Petya Well, he is!

Silence. Alexander taps his foot on the floor.

Ivan Your sole requirements are taking a dump in peace. Get up earlier –

Zhenya Stop being stubborn, Petya.

Petya You're always going on at me to get a job and pay for food and then these freeloaders –

Ivan It was an idea, for Christ's sake!

Kolya takes this moment to speak. He's covered most of his face in burnt cork.

Kolya Does it look like a beard?

Zhenya Bathroom! Now!

Zhenya takes Kolya by shoulder and marches him out to the bathroom.

Petya If she's coming, this P.A. – Clara's moving in and I'm having my bed back.

Alexander (*deaf*) Bad back?

Ivan (*irritated*) Bed back! Bed back!

Alexander Who's Bedbek?

Ivan Forget it! (*To Petya.*) Grow up.

Petya looks stung. Alexander looks at Petya.

Alexander (*kind*) Petya . . . Be grateful. Have some gratitude.
I remember flats with twenty people in them . . . People you hadn't chosen –

Ivan Real shits – Gosha Samarin.

Alexander He couldn't help it. He had a club foot. Our flat had –

Petya (*bored*) Seventeen people.

Alexander Our flats were filled, family, strangers.
Things would go missing, your cigarettes . . . people kept food in saucepans with the lids padlocked on.

Sasha That reminds me, Petya. Stop stealing my fags.

Petya glares at Sasha. Thomas enters, seeing the family all present – he cannot help but briefly glance back to the loo.

Thomas (*breathy*) Hi. Priviet.

All Priviet.

Thomas (*to Sasha*) Hey, everyone's here?!

Thomas sits on the only free space, a small stool at Sasha's feet. It is much lower than first judged, so when sitting down he almost topples backwards. Once perched, his knees are above his ears. Ivan hands Thomas a shot glass of vodka and winks.

Thomas Hey, great stuff – just bang it back in one? Is that what we're doing?

Sasha (*standing*) Has everyone got a glass?

Alexander I don't want to drink any more.

Ivan This isn't a democracy, old man. One more into pissendom!

Thomas looks lost, not understanding what's being said. Sasha raises her glass.

Sasha Okay! – *ras dva tri, sa dnyom razhdeniya* –

Ivan / *Na zdarovye* –

Petya / *Do dna* –

Alexander / *Spasibo!*

Everyone knocks back a shot and then Thomas follows suit.

Ivan Right, I'm getting in the car. Shift yourselves.

Thomas So what's the celebration?

Sasha (*to Tom*) Pardon, what you say?

Ivan exits. Petya looks sullenly at Thomas.

Thomas The celebration?

Sasha His birthday.

Alexander (*depressed*) I better put my coat on . . . Petya.

Petya pulls Alexander out of his chair. They exit. Zhenya enters, crossing their path.

Zhenya Kolya needs his scarf –
(*To Petya.*) What happened to Clara, where's she gone?

Petya We had a row, thanks to you –

Zhenya So she's not coming?

Petya makes an unattractive and disdainful face, and exits after Alexander.

(*Re Tom, thoughtfully.*) And have you, invited your friend?

Sasha (*to Thomas*) Sorry, course – you coming too? Course, it's your choice.

Thomas Oh right, where are you going?

Sasha Restaurant, it's your choice.

Thomas Shall I stay then?

Sasha shrugs.

Zhenya So, did you invite him?

Sasha Yeah, he's got a blister, he doesn't want to come.

Zhenya exits. Sasha is hardly looking at Thomas.

Bye.

Thomas (*nodding*) Yep.

Sasha leaves. Thomas raises his glass to the empty room and the departed troops.
  He sips, the glass is empty. Alexander re-enters and pulls at Thomas's shirt.

Alexander Come.

Thomas It's fine, I've got a lot of work to do.
 . . . Uh, work . . . um, work, lots of stuff –

Alexander Poidyom. Pozhalsta. You're family now.

Alexander leads Thomas out. Fade.

Blackout.

SCENE THREE

Thomas sits on the sofa reading a book. Sasha enters. She stands by the door in silence.

Thomas Hey, are you okay?

Sasha (*mournful*) Going to bed that's all . . .

But Sasha lingers. She stays at the door with a silence growing.

Tom.

Thomas (*smiling*) Yes –

Sasha We must speak . . .

Sasha hesitates.

Thomas Go on.

Sasha mumbles in an almost inaudible monotone. She is blocked from Thomas's view by a large standard lamp with a broad shade.

Sasha I must speak the truth, properly, as friend to friend.

Thomas Okay?

Sasha But it's awful with the world such sad place . . .

Thomas Yeah?

Sasha You're so precious, I stay unopened . . .
This is so sad, too sad –

Thomas Sorry what's . . . what's 'too sad'?

Sasha Things I cannot leave untold. Not for one minute. When you're in front of me – wonderful person, Tom –

Thomas I don't want to interrupt, but it's kind of tricky . . . having this conversation . . . any conversation in fact . . . When you're hiding behind a lamp.

Sasha gulps for air but remains behind the lamp.

Sasha I keep feeling that you want things from me . . .
You cannot expect those things any more.

Thomas At least come where I can see you?

Sasha (*sniffing*) Too sad.

Thomas (*standing*) Please, come here. I won't hurt you.

Sasha timidly comes from her hiding place. She stands in front of him.

Sasha (*firm*) You can't . . . fall in love with me. Tom?

Thomas (*embarrassed*) Yup, okay, no – great, obviously, definitely . . .

His face tells a different story. He sort of looks at the ceiling but not because he's interested in it.

(*Positive.*) Sounds great.

Thomas quickly and unconsciously runs his finger as if moving an invisible sleepy-joe from the corner of his eye.

Sasha You sure?

She fills in the pause.

You go back to England and then . . .
 I agree before, come to Moscow, without thinking or any of that, but I only agreed cos it's you, Tom. Tom who I wish happiness. Whose joy make me joyful . . .
 But now I believe only sadness will stay in me forever.

Thomas Yeah. That's a bit heavy, isn't it? Sort of, sadness forever.

Sasha sits down but not because Thomas asked. She puts her head in her hands.

Sasha Your life's not here. You will leave – so you must stop now.

Thomas runs his hand through her hair.

No! Take me seriously . . .

Thomas Absolutely – no, absolutely.

Sasha bows her head.

Sasha Understand I cannot . . .
The thing in your head – won't happen . . .

Beat.

I'm in love with someone else.

Sasha looks up at Thomas with his face now stranger and changing.

Please *please*, you're most marvellous person, I know this . . . Talking straight, asking things nobody dare . . .
But what can I do when I love someone else?

Thomas (*panicked*) Who're you in love with –?

Sasha He lives in Paris.

Thomas Who is he?

Sasha Brother of friend of mine, his sister's my age . . .
He's older brother, thirty-five –

Thomas And you're a couple?

Sasha Complicate, I kiss him –

Thomas When, fuck it?! – I mean when, sorry?

Sasha (*solemn*) Once, I cannot lie, it was . . . five years ago.

Thomas is confused by this new information.

I don't see him ever, he live in Paris . . . but I cannot stop . . . Love. Love's not about comparing, weighing, making choice.

Thomas I'm sorry, but it is –

Sasha You think it's rational? Counting the plus, minus . . . no, no.

Real love's worse. Real love is when scales can't be used . . .

A place where space has no gravity.

Thomas So forget! He lives in Paris, why don't you just see what happens – I'm here! He's in Paris!

Sasha I didn't decide, fall in love with him, it wasn't my decision . . .

I found out it was so – I wanted to forget. But nothing changes – nothing . . . Even meeting you . . .

Thomas Why didn't you tell me before in an email?

Sasha It can only change itself one day. Not even self-preservation instinct helps me, nothing –

Thomas Okay . . . obviously I sort of get what you're on about, I mean. There's this other guy, you want him and . . . but you can't . . .

Sasha Tom, all night an ambulance wailed in my soul.

Thomas (*wooden*) Yeah okay, great – an ambulance, whatever . . .

Sasha (*passionate*) This is fifth year I try and brainwash donkey heart, still it haven't worked. Understand, of course I see . . . Rationally – you're better option, rationally . . .

Boyfriend of dreams but I find only love as precious friend. With all my will I cannot transfer to other kind . . .

Please understand.

They eye each other, uncertain, awkward in a new silence. Fade.

Blackout.

SCENE FOUR

Morning. The living room is empty. We hear Petya and Clara arguing from offstage. Natalia and Ivan step into the squalid living room. Natalia is in her late twenties, attractive. Natalia puts her small handbag down.

Ivan Pa! Hoi, Dad – hoi! We're back.

Sasha enters, out of breath, dragging Natalia's very large suitcase.

Sasha, clear up some of this crap.

A panting Sasha glowers. Petya and Clara's argument boils over. Natalia looks strained.

Take no notice, they always argue. We continually have these childish squabbles. Sasha, we'll have some tea.

Natalia (*of suitcase, kindly*) God, Sasha, put it down . . .

Kolya enters sleepily.

Ivan Say hello, Kolya –

Natalia Hello, Kolya, do you remember me? I'm Natalia. You came in the office once, I think we stuffed envelopes together . . . Can you remember that? . . . He's quite shy, isn't he?

Ivan (*to Kolya*) Might be an idea to take your hand out of your pants and say hello.

Kolya Hi.

Kolya takes his hand out of his pants and offers it to be shaken.

Ivan (*laughing*) Other hand, Kolya.

Kolya and Natalia shake hands. Alexander enters on Zhenya's arm.

My father Alexander Maximovich. Pa, this is Natalia Borisovna –

Alexander My my, this is Natalia, so it is.

Zhenya embraces Natalia.

Natalia Yevgenya Davidovna –

Zhenya How're you?

Natalia God, I'm so sorry about this, Mama said –

Zhenya (*fanning hands*) We've got plenty of room –

Ivan Sash, stop fussing and get some bloody tea.

Petya and Clara's quarrel reaches fever pitch. Zhenya looks to the door and then to present company.

Zhenya Poor Petya, she's been pecking at him all morning.

Natalia I really only need a few days, honestly, this is great and everything, Ivan –

A china object smashes offstage. It's followed by Clara screaming. Ivan cannot take it any more. He leaps to the door, snarling, and exits.

(*Smiles.*) That's done it.

Zhenya Ivan said the landlord doubled your rent?

Natalia Yeah, that's right, we were paying quite a lot, we were –

But a very physical scuffle is happening offstage, thudding of bodies against walls.

Petya (*from off*) Stop pulling my fucking hair!

Natalia laughs nervously and grins.

Alexander Do carry on –

Zhenya You were saying? Something?

Natalia Yes, so. Yes, the landlord doubled the rent –

We hear Clara howling, thundering footsteps and the front door slamming shut.

Zhenya It's not normally like this.

Kolya Petya, cos Petya hits her.

Zhenya He doesn't. Petya's very gentle, and patient.

Petya (*from off*) You're a fucking whore!

The door opens and Ivan slips back in, grinning.

Ivan Where was I – okay. So. You'll be sleeping in Sasha's bed, if that's okay –

Zhenya And she'll sleep with Kolya.

Sasha On the sofa actually.

Natalia looks worried.

Zhenya Don't be silly, we've got plenty of space. Sasha, show her your room.

Sasha It's only a few days, come on.

Natalia and Sasha exit. The adults wait before they speak. Zhenya stays silent.

Ivan She's just shy.

Alexander I didn't say anything.

Ivan Yeah, I know, she talks a lot, comes across as / a twit.

Alexander Rubbish, hardly said a word.

Zhenya I don't remember her hair being that colour.

Petya enters, looking for his shoes.

Petya, you can't swear at each other like that when we have guests.

Petya Sorry, Mama.

Zhenya It was fucking embarrassing.

Ivan (*kindly*) It was actually quite funny.

Petya continues looking for his shoes, head bowed. Kolya exits.

Petya I need my shoes –

Alexander Clara just needs affection.

Ivan Affection? She needs medication.

Zhenya It's all an act. She's like Sasha, a scratchy cat that needs stroking –

Ivan Is that what they're calling it nowadays?
Petya, she's a cock because she's a miserable person. She really puts the penis in 'happiness'.

Alexander No – she just needs love.

Petya Well there's nothing in the world more off-putting than someone – than someone who's – bloody! – Who's! Where the fuck are my shoes!

Zhenya (*pointedly looking at Ivan*) What's wrong with being needed?

Petya She doesn't need me, she just dumped me.

Zhenya Why?

Petya Cos she did, none of your business. Can't anything be private!

Ivan You want a private conversation, keep your rows down.

Kolya clomps in wearing Petya's oversized shoes.

Petya (*angry*) Kolya!

Kolya (*hurt*) I went and got them for you.

Alexander And that's very nice. Come and sit with Dyedu.

Petya exits without thanking Kolya or putting his shoes on. Alexander strokes Kolya's hair affectionately.

Kolya Play with me. I want to play with the horse on the chess board.

As they too exit . . .

Alexander The problem is this. You can't demand affection. It's like respect – You can hope for it, sometimes you can get it for no reason. But you cannot demand it.

Thomas, Natalia and Sasha enter. Something seems to be irritating Sasha. Natalia is fluent in English, with hardly an accent.

Natalia North London, you know Queen's Park?

Thomas Yeah, I've got a friend, two friends who live in Queen's Park.

Natalia I studied for some times in London – and I notice, it's not all red buses and Buckingham Palace. I notice instead many many Black people, and your metro always slow –

Thomas But that's London Transport, it's crap – So you were, what were you doing –

Natalia Just my studies – learning British life and making friends. Toby? Of course you don't know him – I forget.

Thomas (*mad grinning*) Great.

Zhenya (*to Sasha*) So did she like your room?

But Sasha is watching Thomas and Natalia with rising panic in her eyes.
Zhenya is alert to her daughter's worries.

Ivan (*to Natalia*) You speak English –

Natalia (*to Ivan*) Oh, only a bit, I love the room, Ivan – it's fantastic. I kept saying to Sasha.

Zhenya (*protective*) Thomas is Sasha's friend.

Kolya (*from off*) Mama! Mama! Dyedu's cheating again!

Zhenya exits to Kolya's calling.

Zhenya (*calling, off*) He's old, he can't help it.

Natalia smiles at Thomas.

Thomas (*to Natalia*) Your English is very good.

Natalia Please, I hate my accent.

Sasha Yeah, we've / got to go.

Ivan (*to Natalia*) Do you want some, some tea –?

Natalia Ivan, that would be great. (*To Thomas.*) Are you two staying for tea?

Sasha No, we've got to go –

Thomas Hey, it was such a pleasure to meet you.

Natalia Yeah, I know but I wish my English, I don't practise, so when I studied and did some courses, I was much better. You should've met me then . . . Why don't I show you Red Square sometime –

Sasha Tom, we must, come on –

Natalia (*to Thomas, friendly*) Go . . .
(*Little curtsy.*) Charmed.

Thomas and Sasha exit. Natalia and Ivan stand alone. She smiles.

Ivan When exactly did you learn English?

Fade.

Blackout.

SCENE FIVE

The living room, day. Ivan is on his laptop, working intently.
  His mobile rings. He looks at the caller ID.
  Ivan stands up and looks down the corridor, shuts the door.

Ivan Hello.
  Yeah wait – let me turn the TV on.

Ivan switches the TV on. He flicks through some channels, settles on an old Hitchcock dubbed in Russian. Throughout his phone call the film's soundtrack underscores.

Sure, sure I can talk.

He looks at the door.

Well, it's a weird situation.

He listens.

No. Hold tight.

Beat.

Because I say so.
  Look, I know what I'm doing.

Pause. He goes to the fruit bowl.

No, I'm being silent because I'm thinking.

Pause. He bites into a plum.

No, I'm eating a plum.

He swallows.

Look, what we need to do, is find time to meet and talk properly.
I've told you – *hold tight*. You're being paranoid.

Pause.

Well, that's the way to make it screw up – worrying it's going to screw up.
Of course I'm listening to you –

Petya enters. Ivan panics.

(*Coughing.* Bye now, bye Petya.

Ivan hangs up and puts the phone in his pocket.

Petya Are you okay, Pa?

Beat.

Were you talking to me? Who was on the phone?

Ivan None of your business.

They look at each other.
Ivan turns the TV up, never breaking eye contact with Petya.
The music swells. Fade to black.

Blackout.

SCENE SIX

Petya sits gormlessly staring at his phone. Kolya is wrapped in a towel. Zhenya combs his wet hair with a nit comb.

Kolya But it hurts!

Zhenya Well, I'm sorry, Kolya –

Kolya Don't yank! It hurts!

Zhenya continues, with a slightly lighter touch.

Why can't the bugs just live in my hair?

Zhenya cleans the comb out on a folded piece of loo roll and looks at the 'catch'.

Zhenya Grim.

Kolya Oo, show me, show me grim.

Zhenya holds the loo paper out for Kolya.

Kolya Where's grim?

Zhenya There . . .

Sasha and Thomas enter. They continually touch each other.

Priviet . . . Sasha did you take my Mnogo-dyetnaya Karta?

Sasha It's in your wallet, I put it back.

Kolya Where've you been?

Sasha The zoo.

Petya Made up with the filthy perv?

Sasha and Thomas sit down, together, as a unit. Thomas checks his phone.

Sasha It was actually a lot of fun, we saw loads of animals.

Kolya (*hushed*) He's got an iPhone!

Zhenya Kolya, if you don't sit still, I can't do this –

Sasha (*to Tom*) He wants to play with your iPhone.

Thomas hands him the iPhone.

Don't break it.

Zhenya Kolya – I haven't finished.

Thomas Look I can record you – say something . . .

He presses 'record'.

Hello, Kolya – don't be shy.

Thomas presses 'play'. We hear Thomas's voice: 'Hello, Kolya – don't be shy.'
Kolya grins. The doorbell rings, Zhenya exits.

Sasha Tom's got one week left. What should we do?

Petya Rejoice.

Sasha I was thinking more like taking him out to the country –

Petya And shooting him.

Sasha Do you know anyone with a free dacha?

Zhenya re-enters with an irrational beam on her face.

Zhenya Petya . . . look who's come to see you.

Clara follows in behind her, bashfully.

Clara Oh, the whole gang's here.

Kolya (*perky*) I've got nits.

Clara Cool, lucky you –

Kolya Say something, I wanna record you.

Sasha stands up and hugs Clara.

Sasha How're you?

Clara Hi, Petya.

But Petya is being truculent with his phone.

Zhenya Petya, be nice.

Sasha We'll, um, shall we go . . . Kolya, do you want to interview me next door? Tom.

Everyone exits except Clara and Petya. A brief pause. Clara walks to Petya, trying to be brave – but Petya hasn't even acknowledged her existence. He just stares at his phone like he's really busy.

Clara Petya? What's the matter?

Petya Nothing's the matter, you're the one not speaking to me.

Clara I'm trying to speak to you now.

She hesitates.

I rang you all weekend, but you never picked up?
So I thought I'd just come round.

Petya refuses to look at her and just stares at his phone.

Stop being weird.

Petya I'm not being weird.

Clara Look at me.

Petya looks up, but he's not giving anything away for free.

You're not making me feel very welcome.
I've come to see you and, and you're texting.

Petya Tetris actually.

Clara Oh great, thanks. So you don't want to see me?

Beat.

You didn't pick up any of my calls. You can't just, like, make people disappear –

Petya Really?

Clara Yeah, you can't!

Petya (*stony*) Well –

Clara Well what? You haven't said hello properly, you haven't touched me –

Petya Maybe I didn't wanna give you the wrong impression.

Beat.

Sorry, that came out meaner than I meant.

Petya goes to hug Clara. She pulls away but he insists. She pushes him away.

Clara Why did you delete all your Facebook photos of me?

Petya I didn't.

Clara Okay, well, either you deleted them or you put me on limited profile because I can't see them any more. And you changed your status . . .

For the first time in this scene Petya looks slightly ashamed and uncomfortable.

Clara At least explain what I did?

Petya I dunno – what did *you* do? Who's Igor Shnitkin?

Clara Dick, Petya. Massive dick.

Clara starts gathering her things, muttering, 'Massive dick.' She starts putting her coat back on.

Petya Are you going?

Clara I'm putting my coat on.

Petya This is stupid. Don't go –

Clara Well, I am.

Petya Stupid or going?

Clara stands in her coat, looking angry.

Thanks for coming and seeing me for . . .

Petya glances at his watch.

All of two and a half minutes. I know that can't have been easy . . . you left a T-shirt in my bedroom and some other stuff . . . some hair-straighteners.

A frosty pause.

How's your mum and dad?

A glacial gaze.

Clara I saw your dad on the metro, actually he didn't say hello to me.

Petya (*shrugging*) He was probably busy –

Clara He looked really miserable.

Petya (*smiling*) He works in state finance, it's his job to look guilty.

Clara He didn't look guilty, I said he looked miserable.

Petya Okay, whatever –

Clara No, you're always jumping to conclusions –

Petya You're such a dick.

Clara All I said was I saw your dad on the metro, why're you getting so wound up?

Petya Because you're winding me up.

Clara All I said was I saw your dad.

Petya Again, my dad! Why're you telling me about my fucking dad!
I see my dad everyday, maybe I saw your dad!

Clara You didn't –

Petya But can't you see it's annoying! If you've got something to say, say it! You're mentioning my dad –

Clara Yeah, I haven't got anything to say –

Petya screams with irritation. Clara steps to the door and exits. Petya shouts.

Petya Prick!

Petya can't sit, he gets up, growling. He takes a deep breath and goes to his father's laptop – which is sitting on the table. He opens it, looks at the screen. The prompt for a password comes up. Petya tries to enter one. The 'plink' of a failed attempt. He tries again. Another plink, then another. Ivan comes in, sees Petya with his laptop. Petya starts. They stare at each other.

There's a password on it.

Ivan And why do you think that is?

Blackout.

SCENE SEVEN

Zhenya makes the sofa up for Sasha. She puts two pillows at one end and a blanket. She puts some cornflowers in a jug of water. On the coffee table there is a kettle with two cups. Thomas and Sasha enter.

Zhenya I've put some things out for you.

Sasha Thank you, Mama.

Sasha takes her shoes off.

Zhenya Leftovers in the fridge.

Pause.

Sasha Are you okay?
Is everything okay with Papa?

Zhenya Everything is fine. I've told you to stop worrying about it.

Zhenya kisses her daughter goodnight. Zhenya exits. Sasha pours some boiled water into a cup.

Sasha Our samovar . . . Tsar Nicholas left it to us – I joke. Would you like?

Thomas I can't drink hot drinks. They make me ill.

Beat.

Thanks for today though.

Awkward pause.

Well, 'night then . . .

He turns to leave.

Sasha Aren't you going to kiss me goodnight?

Thomas Oh right, good stuff.

They kiss each other on the cheek, but they linger. Mainly because Sasha holds on to his shoulder.

Sasha (*close*) Cos it's Russian tradition.

Thomas makes a move and they kiss full on. They part, adrenalised.

Thomas English tradition.

Sasha (*raised eyebrow*) You kiss like that in England? I thought you shook hands when you got excite.

Thomas Not always – sometimes we have a snog.

Sasha When you say goodnight to your mothers.

Thomas Actually then, it's a bit more like this.

Thomas kisses Sasha again, slowly walking her backwards on to the sofa. He gently places his hand on her breast and squeezes. His hand moves south and undoes the top button of her jeans. The door swings open and Alexander totally interrupts proceedings. Sasha lunges forward, knocking Thomas away. She is desperate to do her fly up. Alexander doesn't notice them, he's grumbling and moaning, one hand supporting his paunch.

Alexander . . . Charcoal, I need charcoal . . .

Sasha Bad stomach?

Alexander It feels like my heart will break.

He opens a cupboard. Zhenya enters in her dressing gown.

Zhenya That's *wind*. Calm down, let me look.

Zhenya searches. Alexander looks mournful and cradles his aching gut.

Thomas Does he want a Wind-Eze?

He lifts his rucksack up, and pulls a pack of pills out.

It's like flavoured chalk.

He hands the tube to Alexander.

Alexander What is it?

Sasha Makes you fart.

Alexander is unsure. He looks to Zhenya for confirmation that it's okay to take them.

What's the problem?

Zhenya Don't you want to fart now, Alexander Maximovich?

Alexander Well, is that really wise?

Thomas gives Alexander a big smile and thumbs-up. Alexander rather dubiously takes the pills and chews. They watch him.

(*Dogmatic.*) Now I shall sit here.

Sasha Why?

Alexander (*matter-of-fact*) In case I die.

Zhenya You're not going to die. Go to bed.

Alexander No.

Zhenya You're a hypochondriac –

Alexander Only when I'm ill.

Sasha Don't you want some privacy?

Alexander What for? I'll sit here.
 (*Depressed.*) . . . Maybe this, this will be my last winter.

Zhenya Palpable bollocks!

Alexander My father died of heart trouble!

He runs his hands through his hair and finds his glasses perched up top.

And now I'm growing spectacles out of my head.

He puts them on and double-takes. Thomas is wearing a T-shirt, which has 'CCCP' and a large hammer and sickle printed on it.

What's he wearing that for!

Sasha It's a joke, he's being ironic –

Alexander And a swastika, is a swastika ironic?

Thomas Sorry, what?

Sasha He doesn't know what happened –

Alexander Well, explain it to him – I'll explain!

Sasha No, let me explain. (*To Thomas.*) The thing is . . . my grandfather – to him, your T-shirt means in his days –

Sasha's explanation is interrupted. Alexander speaks English in a thick Russian accent, but his desire to be heard and understood pushes him through the language barrier.

Alexander I went, my father died, yes . . . so I must go to the grave –

Sasha He complains father's death.

Alexander I'm seat on bench, looking so, at grave –

Sasha At the graveside, he dropped a cigarette . . . Went bent down to pick it up –

Alexander Macrophone! Macrophone!

Sasha They'd bugged the bench next to his father's grave.

Thomas Why?

Sasha *Pochemu?*

Zhenya Don't go into it, it just works him up.

Alexander Because as I understand they must think the dissidents meet at this place, I, mm . . .

He gestures ripping the microphone up.

Sasha He ripped it out –

Alexander I ripped out, yes, so to return back to KahGehBeh, and bang on door, demanding secret police chief. Desk men ignores – but when them shown what I had to find . . . Sasha, please –

Sasha So he slammed it on desk, 'What do you expect him to say now. He's dead! What can dead people say!' They went crazy, y'know. 'Fuck off! Go on, you shit! Melt like snow.'

Alexander And by this time, on metro afterwards, they already someone reading book by my shoulder.

Sasha Following him.

Thomas absorbs all this.

Thomas Has it changed?

Sasha *Veshchi izmenilis'?*

Zhenya We're talking here, in the flat.
(*To Sasha.*) Explain properly for him in English.

Sasha Mama says before you wouldn't talk in your flat like this.

Alexander People listen in the walls. Bug hidden in the wall – I was, every flat with bugs, it's well to think just the cockroach.
My flat was, with, mm –

Alexander points at the ceiling. Thomas tries to discreetly hide the tea on the table.

Sasha Whenever he was bored he'd go round the room swearing at the ceiling. Pretending infestation of insects.

Alexander shakes his fist at the ceiling.

Alexander We learn better to talk in mystery . . .

Sasha They talked in metaphors, it's called metaphor?

Alexander Metaphors.

Thomas Yeah –

Sasha Everyone talked about sport or art and be really meaning something else.

Thomas Do you think people are listening now?

Pause. Zhenya sniffs.

Sasha No one's listening to us . . .

Beat.

Alexander They come in the middle of the night they came. A knock on the door . . .

Zhenya mimes cutting her throat.

Sasha People vanished –

Thomas Yeah, cos when I was at school we were shown the doctored photographs. You know, where Stalin's airbrushed Trotsky out of the picture.

Sasha Yes, so as if he never existed. One time, one time my grandfather – he was so terrified, the knock on the door, he left the flat and walked the streets.

Alexander (*nodding*) All night I walk.

Sasha They had files on him then.

Alexander They have files on me now.

Zhenya Rubbish.

Zhenya pours another cup of tea and, smiling, gives it to Thomas. Sasha grins.

Thomas Thanks, thank you . . .
(*To Alexander.*) Have you seen your files?

Sasha *Tui kogdanibud' prochyol tvoi KahGehBeh.*

Alexander and Zhenya laugh.

Alexander Files, mm . . . lies, gossiping, mm, half fairy tale.
They accuse you to be spying on the state, mm, the state . . . But when really they spy on you. Old truth, never what people say but why they saying it . . .

Sasha Very hard to translate but like . . . People who say like no smoke without fire, you know this phrase?

Thomas Uh-huh –

Sasha Right, well usually them with matches in their pockets.

Alexander People stop talking, no one was, mm –

Sasha No one was candid –

Alexander Yes, candid, everything became *prostakvasha* –

Sasha A type of sour milk.

Alexander Soviet Union – crazy . . . What's free telephone when there are no private words?
(*Points at ceiling.*) Why stay in if there's always company? This is my communism, freeing of the people.
(*Sighs.*) What great price it cost . . .

Pause.

Sasha Why didn't anyone do anything about it? I went on the anti-Putin march –

Alexander looks anxious.

Alexander Shh shh shh, you don't understand . . .

Thomas (*to Alexander*) Do you like democracy?
(*To Sasha.*) What does he think of it –

Sasha *On sprashivayet pro tepereshnuyu demokratsiyu.*

Ivan enters stage left. He stands unnoticed, listening silently, silhouetted in the doorway.

Alexander (*shrugging*) Put the wrong people in power, expect a car crash.

Sasha We haven't got democracy. What's the choice?

Alexander It is better than it was.

Pause.

I have had a son before Ivan. Nikolai. Kolya.

Zhenya Dyedu . . .

Pause. Alexander sticks his chin out to stop himself crying.

Sasha Our Kolya named after him.

Alexander He was arrested, taken away – arrest boy twelve year old . . .

Beat. Zhenya puts her hand on Alexander's shoulder and rubs.

Sasha (*to Alexander*) Are you okay?

Pause. Alexander can't speak, he points to his voice-box.

Alexander (*quietly*) You explain.

Sasha My grandfather didn't know what to do. Maybe someone was say something. Slowly your whole family gone, like moth in a sweater . . . you understand . . . He was scared for his son but scared for himself, scared for his wife, Anka. He didn't leave the flat for three month. He didn't know who was betray. Maybe even his brothers.

Alexander pulls out his necklace. It's a silver necklace, attached is a small passport photo of a boy.

Sasha When it became safe in 1985, Gorbachev encouraged us to talk about the past. My grandfather had this made – and wears it round his neck to remember Kolya.

Alexander kisses the photograph.

Thomas What happened to Kolya?

Sasha He disappeared. No one saw him again, and no one said a thing.

Pause.

Thomas Oh my God, I'm so sorry.

Alexander I cannot, I couldn't – it was too danger, lucky I am left with one son –

Sasha Spoiled him rotten. That's why he does what he likes.

Alexander (*to Thomas*) Please . . .

Sasha He dreams only one day, he sees him again.

Ivan wordlessly crosses his arms, leaning in the doorway.

Alexander (*to Sasha*) Now tell him to take off that horrible T-shirt.

Thomas What did he say?

Zhenya (*to Alexander*) It's just a T-shirt.

Thomas Sasha?

Alexander stumbles out of his chair and starts trying to take Thomas's T-shirt off.

Thomas Hey!

Sasha (*head in hands*) They don't like your T-shirt. What it represents. Take it off.

Thomas takes off the T-shirt. They smile. Zhenya pats him on the shoulder.

Alexander It's easy today, saying in past, we should have spectacles.

Thomas Hindsight?

Zhenya pulls Alexander out of his chair.

I'm sorry I wore this T-shirt. I had no idea, um. And. Just . . . as a gesture.

Thomas is about to put the T-shirt in the bin.

Alexander Hoi! Whoa!

Zhenya takes the T-shirt and turns it inside out.

Zhenya Worn like this, is okay.

Alexander And now. Is well – to sleep.
Spokoinoi nochi.

Sasha *Spokoinoi nochi.*

Zhenya and Alexander exit to bed, stage right. Ivan stays, still unnoticed . . .
   Sasha and Thomas hardly wait before returning to where they left off.

No one will come now –

Thomas I might.

Sasha kisses Thomas. She touches his crotch, and slowly undoes his flies. Sasha gets on to one knee. Ivan steps forward.

Sasha It's beautiful.

Sasha is about to move the action further when she hears a familiar voice.

Ivan Sasha!

She looks and sees her father stands in the doorway.

Sasha I'm – doing up my shoelace?

Ivan You're not wearing shoes.

Natalia enters next to Ivan. They all look at each other. The lights fade.

Blackout.

SCENE EIGHT

Petya and Sasha stand. Sasha is wearing a grimy apron and yellow washing-up gloves.

Sasha What did you want to say to me?

Pause.

Well what is it?
  You look really shifty, Petya.

Petya I don't look shifty –

Sasha Your eyes are shifty.

Petya My eyes are not shifty, this is so unfair!
  . . . It's very hard not to look shifty when someone is staring at you! I was born with shifty eyes, I've got shifty eyes.

Sasha What have you done?

Petya I haven't done anything.

Sasha Well what is it?

Pause. Petya girds himself. Takes the plunge.

Petya It's happening again . . .
I came in, he was on the phone, and he hung up.

Beat.

Sasha Oh right.

Petya And he looked fucking guilty.

Sasha sits down.

Sasha Did you hear what he was saying?

Petya No. He hung up straight away.

Sasha thinks.

Sasha Did you say anything?

Petya He told me it's none of my business.
I came in, he saw me. Panicked and said 'Bye Petya'.

Sasha You're not the only person in the world called Petya.

Petya rolls his eyes.

Petya No, it's happening again.

Sasha Oh God.

Petya Like last week every time I came in here he slapped his laptop shut like he was looking at porn.

Sasha shrugs like maybe Ivan was looking at pornography.

I checked his history. He's not – and I wouldn't give a shit if he was watching porn. Now he's put a code on his laptop.

Sasha Where is it?

Tom enters with a sly smile on his face.

Thomas Hello, priviet. (*Sultry tone.*) Hello you . . .

Sasha Hi. Are you okay?

Thomas Yes indeedski. Thanks for the gift.

Sasha looks puzzled.

Sasha We're just talking –

Thomas Ah, don't let me stop you.

Beat. Thomas sits next to Sasha. He gives her back a rub.

Sasha Petya?

Petya What.

Sasha Well, what're you going to do?

Petya Nothing. What can I do?

Sasha You could talk to him.

Petya And say what? No, I couldn't.
(*Disdainful.*) Why's he stroking your back like that?

Sasha I have no idea.

Petya Okay.

Pause.

I just don't want it to be like last time.

Sasha Fair enough. Then speak out.

Petya Yeah, I'm all right actually. I quite like my balls in one piece. You speak to him.

Natalia enters.

Natalia God, it's cold out there.

Petya We'll talk later.

Petya exits. Natalia watches him go, curiously.

Natalia (*to Thomas*) How are you? Have you been to Red Square?

Thomas Yeah, it's not really red, is it? I'm great, bit of a headache actually.

Natalia Poor you, let me give you a head massage.

Thomas It's fine, I've taken a pill. It's fine.

Natalia This will actually release the tension. I insist.

Natalia starts to give Tom a very persuasive head massage.

Thomas Please – I mean don't.

But Natalia has Tom's head in her control – he lets out an animal noise, a deep lowing. Sasha looks on.

Oh . . . now, oh now that's . . . that's the bloody spot. Bloody hell.

Sasha looks irritated by this flirtation.

Oh, that's very good.

Natalia (*to Sasha*) You look nice.

Sasha takes off her rubber gloves.

Thomas (*to Sasha, drowsy*) You've got to try this. She's very good.

Natalia I'll do you next.

Sasha (*seething*) Mm . . .

Thomas Where did you learn this?

Natalia Practised on many boyfriends.

Natalia's phone starts ringing. She ignores it and carries on with her head massage.

My mother show me, y'know – foot massage, back massage.

Sasha (*shirty*) Your phone's ringing.

Natalia picks up the phone.

Natalia Hello? Yes. Speaking. Hi. Yeah – he should have had an email.
Let me check . . . one moment.

Natalia mouths to Thomas.

I'll finish you later . . .

Natalia exits.

Thomas What's wrong?

Thomas puts his hand out to Sasha but she is wounded, shrugs him off.

Is it her? Are you saying I should've stopped her –

Sasha What about get up – walk away.

Thomas Why?

She glares at him.

Right. Yeah, no – yeah. You're right.
I should've, exactly – sorry.

Beat. Thomas is confused by Sasha's disproportionate reaction.

But – I loved your gift . . .

Sasha (*puzzled*) What?

Half-beat.

Thomas You sexy person.

Thomas touches the end of her nose with an outstretched index finger. He takes out a leopard skin print thong out of his pocket, and inhales deeply.

God, they still smell of you.

Sasha (*incensed*) They're not mine.

Thomas What?

Sasha They're not mine –

Thomas (*smelling again*) Are you sure?

Sasha Yes! Don't be so disgusting.

Thomas But – but you left them in my bed? Under the pillow?
Maybe they're – there's always a logical explanation.

Thomas steps forward. He wants to make up with Sasha, but seeing the thong in his hands, she turns on her heel and exits, calling out:

Sasha Petya. Petya!! Come here.

Petya reluctantly re-enters with Sasha. Sasha turns to Thomas.

I need to speak to my brother. Alone.

She takes the thong off him.

Thomas Have I done something wrong?

Sasha Please.

Thomas goes out. Sasha shows Petya the thong.

Is this Clara's?

Petya How should I know, I don't wear her pants.
It's not hers – she can't wear thongs, they give her thrush.

Sasha Tom found it in his bed, your bed –

Petya Yeah, my bed, he's sleeping in my bed and I'm on the floor!

Sasha We're not talking about the bed situation – go on, I can tell there's more.

Petya There isn't more. I told you about the phone call and the code on the laptop and I told you about the underground.

Sasha No you didn't, what about the underground –

Petya Clara said she saw him on the underground –

Sasha You look really scared?

Petya I just don't want you to shout at me . . . Clara saw him and Papa pretended not to see her.

Sasha thinks a bit.

Sasha Maybe he didn't see her.
That's not really evidence, Petya.

Petya wrestles with himself a moment.

Petya And I read an email. From someone. In his email.
And it said stuff about they needed to meet and discuss and that the situation couldn't go on like this . . .

Pause. Sasha is shocked.

Sasha Who was it from?

Petya Um. It was some googlemail account but this was before he put the password on –

Sasha When did you read the email?

Petya Two months ago. And then I looked again the other day.

Sasha Two *months* ago! Why didn't you tell me?

Petya Because I didn't want *this* to happen.

Sasha Petya. So you just covered for him.

Natalia comes in.

Petya No I fucking didn't!

Natalia Sorry – should I go?

Petya We've finished, it's fine.

Sasha We haven't finished, Petya.
  I can't believe you sat on this for two months and didn't tell me!

Petya Well, what would you have done!

Natalia What's happened?

Petya Nothing. Something to do with Papa.

Petya looks at Sasha and shakes his head 'no'. Stalemate. Sasha breaks it.

Natalia That's none of my business.

They look at her. Pause.

Sasha I just want to know who it is!
  I think we should ask him?
  It's just what's the best way.

Natalia's thoughts seem elsewhere. She starts texting. Petya and Sasha are psyching themselves up.

If we sat him down and just asked outright . . .
  'Who is it?' You know we just go, 'Who is it –?'

Petya Yeah, we just go –

Sasha 'Who is it!'

Petya 'Who the fuck is it!'

Sasha Yes! Exactly! –

Petya And you ask him.

Sasha has hysterical giggles. Natalia looks up from her phone and then goes back to texting.

Sasha No no no!

Petya Yes yes yes! It's better coming from you.

Petya and Sasha momentarily try and calm down.

Sasha Look, he tramples over all of us, we never stand up to him. I really really think it should be you.

Petya Oh really –

Sasha Yeah, it's always me . . . seriously . . .
Petya, I promise if you start the ball rolling –

Petya I'll be behind you all the way . . .

Natalia smiles, and shakes her head in disbelief.

(a) You have a better relationship with him.
 (a) You can actually talk to him.

Sasha So this might be really good for your relationship.

Petya What're you talking about?! It would be terrible for my relationship, that's why I want you do it.

A phone bleeps, Petya pulls out his phone.

Sasha It's Clara?

Petya shakes his head 'no'. The phone bleeps again. Natalia reaches for her own phone.

Natalia (*dumbly*) My phone?

Sasha But it's coming from over there.

Ivan's mobile is jiggling on the sofa. Something like panic seems to cross Natalia's face.

He left his phone, he's left his phone!

Sasha walks over and picks up the phone.

Petya What does it say?

Natalia (*beaming*) Guys – come on, is that really the right way to behave?

Sasha Yep. (*Reading out loud.*) 'Call me.' That's all it says.

Petya No way – who's it from?

Sasha This number, called 'R' – were the emails from someone called 'R'?

Natalia (*disapproving*) Should you really read your dad's messages?

Sasha and Petya stop to think.

Sasha Yes, yeah – I think so, actually, under the circumstances . . .

She looks back at the phone, engrossed. Natalia seems to be fiddling with her phone in her pocket, switching it off.

Sasha Oh my God! There are fucking loads of them –

Petya You see! I told you. What do they say?

Sasha They don't say anything – it's just like . . .

She reads off the screen. Natalia looks uncomfortable.

Sasha 'Eight o'clock. Flying Dutchman.'

Petya That's a restaurant – the Flying Dutchman, I've eaten there, it's shit. Call the number.

Natalia Guys. This could be much bigger than you think. Your dad works for the government, it could be something important . . .

Sasha (*disbelieving*) Really?

Natalia looks enigmatic.

Natalia Yes . . . why not?

Sasha Because it's Papa, he's a pussy – is he doing something illegal?

Natalia No. I don't know. I don't think so –

Sasha Then why did you say . . . do you know something about his work?

Natalia (*firmly*) No, I'm not important enough. I just think you shouldn't be snooping, this could be really important.

Petya That stuff doesn't go on any more.

Natalia It does.

Beat.

Sasha We thought it was a woman. I'm going to call it.

Sasha looks dubious and is about to call the number when Natalia snatches the phone from Sasha.

Natalia All right, I'll do it. I work with him yeah, then if . . .

Natalia presses call and holds the phone to her ear.

(*To the others.*) 'This is the Megafon messaging service. The person you're calling is unable to take your call.'

Sasha (*interested*) Your hand's shaking.

Natalia (*finger over mouth*) Shall I leave a message?

Sasha / No

Petya Yes –

Sasha No! – We need the upper hand.

Natalia hangs up and stands quivering.

. . . Okay, what do we do now?

Petya Yeah.

Sasha We're stronger as a team, I'll back you up.

Petya Why do we even wanna do this –

Sasha He's gotta stop doing this, Petya. You're being a wimp.
Fucking talk to him tonight.

Petya I can't – what do I say?

Sasha You just say, you just go . . .

But Sasha is lost for words.

Petya See! It's impossible!

Natalia (*hopeful*) I could do it –

They look at her. Sasha looks baffled.

Petya (*relieved*) Oh that'd be great –

Sasha Petya! She's our guest. It's got nothing to do with her.
I'm fed up with this sneaking around.
(*Bullying tone.*) Petya!

Petya I'll do it then, I'll do it!
But not cos I wanna fucking do it.

He paces, getting himself into the role . . .

Sasha You've gotta just think of it as – like the first step of adulthood.
It's unfortunate, but you have to talk him.

Petya Yup. Yeah. I have to do this. I just have to talk to him.
Are you sure I have to?

Sasha (*firm*) Yes. Tonight. He'll be back for supper at seven.

Petya Oh God . . . I don't think Kolya should know, do you?
(*To himself.*) Kolya can't find out.
What about Mum?

Sasha Mama has to know, but later –

Petya Do I have to do her as well?

Sasha (*fiercely*) Yes.

She watches the uncomfortable Petya.

(*Praising.*) You're being so mature, Petya.

Petya (*lofty*) Well I suppose, well, when your parents behave like children – what else can you do? You have to be the adult.

Ivan enters.

Ivan (*muttering*) Priviet.

Sasha, Natalia and Petya jump out of their skins.

Petya Papa!

Ivan All right?

Petya Fine fine, I just wasn't expecting you.

Sasha How was your day, Papa?

Ivan sits down on the sofa, takes out his laptop and tries to switch it on.

Ivan (*speaking to laptop*) Come on.

Petya What's happened, Papa?

Ivan My laptop broke and . . . I lost all my work.

Petya mimes cutting his throat to Sasha. She looks back, vehemently disagreeing. Natalia is stuck in the middle. Ivan looks up at Petya.

Petya (*blankly*) Just your laptop broke . . . ?

Ivan Yes?

Petya Well, nothing.

Natalia Do you want me to call Dmitri, in IT?

Ivan tries to turn it on again, in the vain hope that it might come back to life.

Ivan Working perfectly normally, and then I pressed 'save'. I pressed – uh God . . . and the, the spinning . . . Y'know, beachball of death . . . and the whole eighteen-thousand word document vanished.

Ivan stares at the screen, waiting for something, anything to happen.

(*More to himself.*) Oh come on.

Ivan looks at his children. They're smiling. Ivan smiles right back at them, clueless of their intentions.

Ivan Why're you grinning, what's so funny?

Petya Nothing.

Ivan Sodding things got Parkinson's.

Sasha and Petya's smiles grow bigger. Petya leans over to see what's going on with the laptop.

(*To Petya.*) Stop jiggling next to me . . .
It's like you've got worms –

Sasha and Petya snigger.

Go and wipe your arse.

Sasha and Petya laugh. Ivan, bemused, smiles at his laughing children. Natalia is not laughing.

Ivan Seriously . . . what's so funny?

Petya Nothing, nothing – we're just being silly.
And you're being funny.

Sasha (*with intent*) Petya, Papa –

Petya (*mouthing*) No! Fuck off –

Sasha Papa, Petya has something to say.

Pause. All eyes on Petya.

Ivan Well get on with it – you a poof or something?

Petya Yep.

Zhenya comes in, catches the tail end of this, stops in surprise.

Zhenya Petya?

Sasha *Petya –*

Petya No Sasha, I'm gay.

Ivan frowns, with a puzzled smile: what's going on?

Petya Yep, gay, that's all.

Natalia (*from nowhere*) You're having an affair.

Beat. Ivan is stunned.

Zhenya What're you talking about?

Sasha Is it true?

Pause.

Petya (*stammering*) Who is she?

Beat.

Sasha Is it true?

Ivan looks at Natalia.

Ivan (*blank*) Yes.

Blackout.

Act Two

SCENE ONE

Early evening in the living room. A family summit has been called. Everybody is present except for Kolya, Thomas and Natalia. Alexander breaks the silence.

Alexander Can I speak? Is that alright?

Zhenya Alexander Maximovich, please, feel free. All I meant was we must all take our turns . . .

Petya You wanted to say something, Dedushka?

Alexander We're all talking about a resolution, and I'm just wondering if the cure might be closer to home . . . I mean, when I was in the navy, a common cure for the desperate man was – whores.

Ivan Yeah, I'm not seeing a prostitute, Pa.

Alexander Why? You might find it a beneficial sort of – release of stress?

Ivan Well, you bloody go then –

Alexander Ivan, I'm too old. I can't hear people talking and my heart . . .

He momentarily contemplates seeing a prostitute at his age.

Still, I mean, my heart, it'd be ridiculous. I mean if you're not interested tell me to shut up –

Ivan Shut up.

Alexander So quick to turn your nose up! It's a terrible habit. The women are hard working and . . . charming?

Very charming, I was in the navy and this one girl. She didn't have a leg – amputated, you see. She could joke about it. She saw it was ridiculous, but she had a sense of humour.

Zhenya Alexander Maximovich –

Alexander I haven't finished, Yevgenya Davidovna. (*To Ivan.*) Give me one good reason. I'll pay, happily . . . Ivan, these girls can be quite something sometimes and when they . . . don't have a leg perhaps . . . just remember you don't look at the chimney when you're poking the grate.

Ivan Can we have a serious conversation now?

Beat.

First off – let's be completely clear here . . . there isn't a problem. We don't need a solution. Everything's bloody fine the way it was. So stop meddling. We're happy.

The present company don't seem quite persuaded.

(*Forceful.*) We're happy! It's this endless 'oh maybe he should see a prostitute', 'maybe he should have a vasectomy'.

Present company look amongst themselves, nodding and murmuring 'Vasectomy . . .'

I'm not having a vasectomy!

Zhenya Okay, so I think we need to communicate, openly and frankly.

Ivan is unchanging, unapologetic, and doesn't drop his guard. Zhenya looks wounded but gearing up for the fight ahead.

There are a lot of things here . . . coming into the open, a lot of emotions . . . People feel hard done by, Ivan.

Zhenya looks at her husband but he is eyeing the distance.

Maybe . . . Ivan?

Ivan looks at his wife.

I think we need family therapy.

Ivan Family what?

He shakes his head in disbelief, thins his lips and grinds his teeth.

Zhenya Sasha spoke to Thomas and he said that in England when problems arise –

Ivan What the fuck's she talking to him about it for?!

Sasha They speak to someone who is trained in resolving family issues –

Ivan (*dangerous*) This is a family matter –

Sasha Which is why it's called family counselling, Tom said –

Ivan Course he said that, he's English.

Sasha Clara said the same thing, and she's not English –

Ivan Well, she wishes she was, she's like every Russian nouveau-riche arsehole –

Sasha That's not fair, it was her cousin who went to one. There's a centre and you talk to a woman –

Ivan And they write it all down and pass it on to the authorities.

Zhenya It's not like that any more.

Ivan Bullshit. How do you know what they do with what they hear? They do what they want. We don't talk

about this to other people – it's a family matter. It stays in these four walls.
What'd a therapist do – they don't know us, we know ourselves better than anyone else.

Sasha That's the whole bloody point, that they don't know you . . .

Ivan This is a family problem, it stays private – the state *don't* get involved.

Zhenya Fine, and so we've clearly all made mistakes, myself included.

Ivan Horseshit, what did you do?

Zhenya Nothing! I didn't do anything, but there is a problem. It needs . . .
I just think, there's room for discussion, talking, big issues –
Must be aired, for any type of resolution . . .

Ivan stares at the ceiling.

This might be useful, Ivan.

Ivan You know what happens when you publicise family matters, yeah? So go, if you want, but kindly count me out.

Sasha Then it isn't family therapy. We need to go as a family, all of us.

Ivan Stop! Behaving like a little Tsarina –

Zhenya People need to voice opinions, Ivan –

Sasha As a family group, in a safe place –

Ivan This is a safe place! Who's scared to speak?

Silence.

Zhenya Ivan . . . You can be quite intimidating, we all need to be able to talk without worrying about the consequences –

Alexander What will you agree to? I offer to pay for you to get help –

Ivan A whore! You said I should see a prostitute!

Alexander (*to Zhenya*) The girls rarely enjoy themselves.

Zhenya Yes, I think we're all talking about the same thing.

Sasha But it needs to be for all of us. A room where we all . . . feel safe to speak.

Ivan This is a room . . . what? This is suddenly not a room –

Zhenya Of course this is a room but –

Ivan No no, feel free to chat amongst yourselves.

A hesitation. Zhenya's nervous sniffing is the only sound we hear.

Zhenya When you look so stern. It's very hard to be honest with you.

Silence.

Ivan I think the truth is no one's really got anything to say.

Beat. Zhenya nervously sniffs again.

Stop sniffing – blow your nose!

Alexander Ivan!

Sasha (*to Ivan*) Who is she?

Petya (*to Sasha*) Can I have a cigarette?

Sasha No. (*To Ivan.*) Who is she?

Petya ignores Sasha's question and lights up one of her cigarettes.

Ivan Who she is has nothing to do with any of you. It's an irrelevance to this conversation.

Sasha Well, it isn't because you're having an affair with her.
So she's part of it too . . .

Ivan You don't know what you're meddling with, you don't know the full extent –

Sasha So tell us!

Ivan I'd rather not.

Sasha (*sarcastic*) Why – to protect us? Or so we can't judge you?

Thomas enters – heads turn at bovine speed, and he is met with the furrowed brows of the family.

Thomas Is my phone charger . . . ?

He picks up his bag – and starts to riffle through it, pulling out the contents quickly . . . metro cards, magazines, sweet wrappers etc.

The charger should be in here . . .

Sasha butts in.

Sasha No – please! Take bag out.

Thomas tries to put the magazines, sweet wrappers, metro cards etc. all back in at once – but they don't fit so easily . . .
Ivan sighs. Thomas turns tail.

Thomas Priviet, I mean poka . . . *prat.*

He exits, Ivan pulls an expression – the self-satisfied schoolmaster.

Ivan As we're airing things, what about him? Why don't we talk about that situation for a minute.

Beat.

Mm, funny, you're not having such a great time now –

Sasha He is a friend –

Ivan With an erection. For Christ's sake, what d'you take us for, Sasha –

Sasha crosses her arms.

I don't know why you're crossing your arms . . .

Sasha (*coldly*) Who is she?

Ivan Let me explain something to you. You're making a very simple mistake here, which is this: you seem to think I'm answerable to you.

Sasha You didn't have an affair with yourself.
There was someone else – we need to know who she is . . . (*Faltering.*) To understand what happened . . .

Ivan slowly holds up his index finger to his lips. Sasha grows silent.

Ivan (*slowly and clearly*) What don't you understand? You seem so certain you know what happened –

Sasha We don't. You haven't told us.

Ivan What can't you answer for yourself? You're an adult, aren't you?

Sasha nods.

(*Steely.*) Good. Now listen to me. Forget about it.

Silence. After a moment Sasha opens her mouth but that's as far as she gets.

The fact of the matter is, this is between your mother and me.

Sasha But you're not telling her either. She said –

Zhenya Sasha . . .

Ivan (*coldly*) So you've *all* been talking about this?

Zhenya can't answer.

It has nothing to do with you. I love my children very much.
   I would've thought that much was obvious. Sure Petya's gay – but I still love him.

Petya Yeah, I'm gay.

Zhenya Petya's not gay.

Alexander (*touching Petya*) I'm sure you'll make some young man very happy.

Sasha looks at her father, and he looks right back at her.

Sasha Why can't you say it was a mistake? And that you're sorry.

Zhenya Because he's not going to stop seeing her, he does what he wants.

Ivan No, the mistake was you found out – I have a pudeur about discussing this.

Sasha Because you're ashamed.

Ivan No! The truth is, people have affairs – get real, I'm not about to pretend I'm sorry I did it, I'd be lying –

Sasha So lie! Lie! Lie for us – this is your opportunity. Acknowledge what you did was wrong. (*Desperate.*) You could say things –

Ivan I'm not about to say. I love you, but I will not be held hostage to sentimentalism. You can't tell me how to behave . . .

Zhenya How can you be like this? So uncompromising?

Ivan I apologised!

Sasha When!

Ivan Just then, fuck it! What do you want – a signed confession, walk around in a hair shirt whipping myself? I mean I feel completely unapologetic.

Zhenya is the one to shake her head and grind her teeth this time.

Let's get some things straight, okay – I'm bored of being portrayed as some despot. I'm not about to leave your mother, right. I'm not about to run into the sunset because *nothing's changed*. We're a family and we stick together but raking over things, picking off the scab –

Sasha So you're saying you want to have secrets –

Ivan No, I'm saying some things are private. This is none of your business. I'm not affecting anyone but myself.

Sasha No, we're a family.
   If you lie to Mama, you're lying to all of us –

Ivan Why does everything have to be in the open? Ahhh, for Christ sake, I mean I can't believe it! If you just gave it time –

Zhenya (*ironic*) Oh, give it time –

Ivan Yes! Time! Time! Let it heal. Talking and constant discussion is a mistake –

Sasha That's convenient –

Ivan It's destructive, believe me. We've been talking for forty minutes and we've only made things worse. Left alone with a little time this will heal. End of conversation.

Alexander looks in pain, he fiddles with a molar in his mouth.

Petya What's wrong?

Alexander Toothache.

Ivan Yeah, well, maybe you should see a prostitute.

Ivan stands up and starts to exit.

Screw this –

Zhenya Where are you going?

Ivan For a walk.

He exits.

Sasha What's he doing?! Stop him, Mama!

Zhenya What's the point? We can't do anything –

Sasha We haven't finished, tell him to come back.

Petya takes another cigarette.

Stop stealing my fags and follow him!

Petya is immobile. Sasha stands up: she will follow Ivan then.

Zhenya Sasha, let him be –

Alexander Spying on people isn't the solution, let him walk it off and come back in his own time . . . Has anyone a pain killer? My tooth's really throbbing.

Sasha Petya, go, hurry up – Petya!

Petya Can I have a cigarette?

Sasha NO – just go!

Petya reluctantly gets to his feet and exits. Sasha turns on her mother.

Why don't you ever stand up for yourself?! Why don't you ever tell Papa what you *really* think – stop censoring yourself the whole time –

Zhenya Shut up! Stop it! It's as bad as him, you're bullying me – it's exhausting. I'm tired . . . Can we stop arguing?!

Alexander hugs Zhenya.

Now he thinks we talk behind his back.

Sasha We do. It's very hard to talk about him to his face. We just saw.

Zhenya He's very paranoid.

Sasha Because he does bad things.

Zhenya This wears me down –

Sasha I know it wears you down – that's why I want you to do something about it properly, why can't you just tell him –

Zhenya Because! The second I try and speak to him, he loses his temper. The last time this whole business happened I tried talking to him and he told me to wait – He said, 'Be patient, time's a great healer,' so I've waited a year – and it's exactly the same.

Sasha Talk to him! Like I said! You're still not telling him how you're feeling. It's shit! He needs to know – *leave* him!

A stunned silence from Zhenya and Alexander.

Papa takes you for granted. Show him that it's not all one way. You need him to see that he can't . . . Show him what the alternative is like.

Zhenya This has been going on for years – when *I* met *him* he was with someone else. The same thing happens again and again. We never put it right. It just repeats.

Beat.

Sasha Don't let him get away with it.

Zhenya Papa'll just say I'm being ridiculous! I should forget about it. 'Everything is fine, isn't it? What's wrong now?!' He makes me so miserable, I just end up wishing I could make him suffer.

Alexander That is no solution, Yevgenya Davidovna.

Zhenya You're right, but if it's not candid it can't be a relationship.
  Aii, so I clear my mind and try and speak calmly . . . and we get nowhere. He wants it to fester, and I'm suffocating.
  I suppress what I feel and feel I'm drowning, because I know talking only annoys him.

Sasha So what're you going to do? Are you going to talk to him?

Zhenya No. (*Resigned.*) I'll wait. I'll grit my teeth.
  If time's a great healer I better be patient.

The lights fade.

Blackout.

SCENE TWO

Natalia and Sasha wait for Petya's return. It's late and Sasha yawns.

Natalia Go to bed, you look tired.

Sasha looks at Natalia.

Your dad's just drinking himself stupid somewhere.

Sasha You don't know that, what if he's with her?

Natalia Well. You still need to sleep. It's after two.

Sasha stands up, yawns and stretches. She looks at Natalia.

Sasha Y'know, we thought it was you . . .
The one Papa was seeing.

Natalia (*smiling*) Oh right, it's not me by the way.

Sasha Are you sure?

Natalia Yes! Sasha –

Sasha Yeah. I can see it's not.

Natalia raises an eyebrow, she's inquisitive.

I just can. You're not the type. You're a wimp.

Sasha sits down and plays with a mousetrap. Setting it and releasing it – snap!
Natalia speaks tentatively.

Natalia Did I do something?

Sasha No – is it, like, someone at work?

Natalia If it was someone at work, I'da told you.

Sasha (*impish*) Why?

Natalia Because y'know – you have a right to know.

Sasha Is that why you said to Papa, 'You're having an affair'?

Natalia You had a right to know.

Sasha looks at her cynically and then sets the mousetrap. She opens a big bag of crisps on the table and carefully puts the mousetrap in the bag. She smiles at her handiwork.

Sasha I keep trying to imagine how it'd happen. And I feel I can sort of see, now. He's funny – that's the key, isn't it? Oh come on, he is! I've seen him make you laugh –

Natalia He's funny –

Sasha So, he makes her feel . . . comfortable, barriers blur . . . You're talking about work and then he's mentioning your boyfriend –

Natalia I don't have a boyfriend –

Sasha (*impatient*) I'm not talking about you, I'm imagining . . . Like I had to do an essay with this guy, it didn't take long before we were flirting. And I mean I never found him attractive before, actually – kinda ugly. Squinty . . . before I knew it we're chatting about sex – it's a more interesting conversation, isn't it?

She shakes her head and thinks.

Do you think that happens before or after you start having drinks?

Natalia (*guarded*) We have work drinks but Ivan's never alone.

Sasha plays her silent card. A pause grows.

Sasha You're the only girl in the office –

Natalia No, there are some women. Typists.

Sasha But when I googled the office, everyone else was a man.

Beat.

Natalia Why don't you just say what you're thinking!

Pause.

Yeah, well, I'm offended, I'm going to bed. And I think you should go too.

She stands up. Sasha holds out a packet of cigarettes, offering Natalia one.

Sasha You want one?

Natalia You put match heads in them.

Sasha Yeah . . . Petya steals everything. I swear if Petya was a girl he'd be wearing my thong . . .

A pause. Then Sasha holds out the thong Tom found, and drops it on the sofa.

It's yours.

Natalia (*definitive*) No it's not, Sasha.

Sasha Then why was it in Tom's bed?

Natalia I have no idea, you tell me . . .

Sasha Tom found it in his bed and thought it was mine.

Pause.

His room's the only one with a lock. And it's empty all day.

Silence. Natalia is seething.

So forget about it, it's not yours and we're family.

Natalia Why do you hate me?

Sasha I don't hate you.

Natalia Then why're you being like this?

Sasha (*shrugs*) Aren't you going to bed?

Beat.

Natalia Are you angry about something? Are you unhappy?

Sasha (*cool*) I'm very happy.

Natalia Coulda fooled me, you don't sound happy. Or look happy.

Sasha Because no one's actually ever really happy, are they?

Natalia I've been happy here, in your home. I've been very happy.

Sasha But it doesn't really exist – happiness? The promise. True-blue blissful happiness.

Natalia thinks for a moment.

Natalia I loved someone. That was happiness.

Sasha How do you know?

Natalia Cos when I think about it I'm sad.

They sit thinking about this. Natalia watches Sasha, Sasha is working overtime, trying to work out who 'it' could be.

(*Light-hearted.*) Your dad – we've been having this thing.

Sasha stares at her. Natalia gives a smile showing she's joking.

Oh come on, Sasha! It was my first boyfriend, at school. Mitya. No offence, I wouldn't touch your dad with a barge pole. Not my type, I mean sweet, but . . . married to his – penis.

Sasha looks slightly stung.

Was that offensive?

Sasha shifts her weight. The comment was clearly meant to be offensive.

Sasha I'm going to bed.

Natalia doesn't quite understand.

This is where I've got to sleep. Can you go, please?

Natalia stands up and starts to exit. She stops and stands by the door.

Natalia Sasha. I don't want to leave things like this.

Sasha Why not?

Natalia No, I'm sorry. I shouldn't have let you wind me up, you're younger than me – accept my apology.

Sasha Don't patronise me.

Natalia Stop talking into your pillow.

Sasha lifts up her head.

Your dad cares about you, I work with him, he adores you. Do you know how many clients he boasts to about you guys? People make mistakes. Forgive him.

Sasha He has to stop for that to happen.

Natalia We do things we know are wrong, regret them, and carry on doing them.

Sasha takes a 'spiked' cigarette out of the packet, but she doesn't light it.

Sasha Yeah, well, I don't. And I want to go to sleep now.

Beat. Natalia decides to take the plunge.

Natalia Tom adores you, he loves you and you want to end it –

Sasha End what? I'm not married to Tom, yeah? I didn't have children with him. I didn't make any promises, okay . . . I can put my 'foreign affair' on hold.

Natalia He still loves you though.

Sasha (*hard*) Then stop flirting with him. He's mine.

They stare at each other. There is an audible knock at the front door. They are startled. Whoever is at the front door thumps it twice, loudly. Both girls are scared. They play high emergency, whispering –

Natalia Who's that?

Sasha Who is it?

Natalia Should we open it?

Sasha (*shaking her head 'no'*) We don't know who it is –

Natalia I'm sure it's just Petya.

Sasha Petya's –
(*Hoarse whisper.*) Bloody Petya's got bloody keys . . .

Natalia (*whispering back*) What's wrong?

Sasha I'm just worried it's – the police. They picked up two more boys for not doing conscription.

Natalia looks at her watch.

Natalia The police wouldn't come round in the middle of the night, would they?

The bell rings. Short and sharp.

Sasha Petya wouldn't ring the bell. He knows it'd scare Dedushka.

They stare at each other, scared. Unsure what to do. Natalia takes the bull by the horns and starts to exit. Sasha follows her. They creep out of the room. A painful moment passes – they re-enter with Petya.

Sasha (*angry*) Why haven't you done anything about it! It's a treasonable offence if you don't have a proper reason –

Petya You could've answered the door and told them I wasn't in –

Sasha Petya, that's fucking shit – *do* something about it! We thought it was them –

Petya Ahh, I am! I'm seeing the doctor tomorrow. I've got an appointment first thing. Just leave me alone.

Sasha looks disbelieving.

Sasha So? Where was Papa? Did you find him?

Petya He did exactly what he said he was going to do . . . I caught up with him at the bridge –

Sasha Did he see you?

Petya No, I just watched him. He watched this gay brass band playing. For an age. I'm not doing it again, Sasha, do your own dirty work. It feels shit spying on him like that –

Sasha Didn't stop you monitoring Clara's email.

Petya I didn't –

Sasha You told me you read all her emails.

Natalia (*shocked*) Petya!

Petya I was trying to help her. She kept saying how miserable she was in her emails to this Shnitkin dick and he kept emailing her back – so I sort of deleted his emails, mm . . .

Beat. Natalia is shocked.

Yeah, then had to delete them from the deleted mail, cos she might've seen that – I'm genuinely not proud of myself.
   (*To Sasha.*) I wish I hadn't told you about it now.

Petya puts his feet up on the couch.

Sasha Well you did – don't put your feet on my pillow. They stink.
   . . . So what happened?

Petya When?

Petya turns the television on. We hear the Russian presenter, but it's on low volume.

Sasha Tonight, with Papa!

Petya Nothing, he went to a bar and . . .

Petya is distracted by the television.

And some woman came in and they kissed –

Sasha He kissed another woman?!

She turns the television off to get Petya's attention.

You saw him kissing her –

Petya (*slow*) Not a sexy kiss, only hello . . .

Sasha But you think it was her –

Petya Well, how should I know?!

Sasha Cos he was kissing her! What did she look like!?

Natalia Was she fatter, was she fat?

Petya Old skinny woman . . . looked a bit like a woodpecker. And then they like kissed hello. I think she worked at the bank with him, remember the one who, she always sent us chocolates for Christmas.

Sasha She's KGB.

Petya She's not, that was her sister.

Petya sticks his hand into the bag of crisps, setting off the mousetrap. Screaming, he pulls his hand out of the bag at double speed. Face shocked, eyes watering – he sees his laughing sister.

Why?

Sasha You kept nicking my stuff . . .

Petya You're such a twat-face – we're his children, it's got fuck all to do with us. Nothing! We can't do anything! Spying on him is bonus, I'm not gonna be your KGB . . . (*Rubbing his hand.*) Apologise.

Sasha No. It was a joke.

A forgetful Sasha puts the infamous cigarette back in her mouth. She thinks, takes the cigarette out of her mouth.

Get a sense of humour.

Sasha puts the cigarette in her mouth and lights up – flames shoot out. She whinnies, and throws the cigarette away from herself – then stamps on it. Petya has hysterics.

Petya Seriously, just get a sense of humour, Sasha . . .

Petya carries on laughing.

Sasha It singed my hair. It's not funny.

Thomas enters. He leads Kolya, who's been crying. They're wearing pyjamas. Kolya drags his pillow behind him. Everyone sobers up.

Thomas I heard him crying, I didn't know what to do.

Kolya (*adamant*) I'm not going school tomorrow. Okay.

Petya picks up his little brother. He's much heavier than expected.

Petya Jeez, whoa – you've got heavy.

Sasha leans over Petya's shoulder and puts her arms round both of them. They rock back and forth and when they speak it's a soft lulling, pigeons cooing . . . Tom and Natalia watch.

Petya/Sasha Kolya, Kolya / Kolya.

Kolya Petya, I'm scared –

Petya Don't be scared, what're you scared of –

Kolya Had a nightmare, cos the men came for me, Dyedu's crying, they wanted to carry me away –

Petya Y'know what I think happened, I think cos I rang the front door, I forgot my keys –

Sasha Silly Petya.

Petya And that's why you had a weird dream.

Kolya But what about someone hiding in the ceiling, when I woke up I saw a face staring at me.

Sasha No –

Petya You just imagined that.

Kolya Are you sure?

Sasha Yes, when has that ever happened?

Beat.

Kolya 'Kay.

Thomas (*to Sasha*) Is everything okay?

Sasha Yes. Go to bed.

Petya (*to Kolya*) You've got loads of friends at school –

Kolya 'Kay.

Petya You love school. Everything's okay –

Kolya breathes hesitantly.

Kolya But is it?

Sasha Why don't you sleep with me? Natalia can sleep in here, and we can sleep in my bed, like when you were little. Do you remember how you'd pretend to be my little brown bear?

Kolya Mm.

Sasha You're just tired. Let's go to bed.

Kolya nods his head and tucks it in to Petya. The three siblings exit. Thomas watches Natalia from the doorway. She is crying, silently.

Thomas Good night

Natalia doesn't look back.

Natalia Yes.

*But Thomas doesn't leave, he watches her – as she puts the thong in her pocket.
The lights fade.*

Blackout.

SCENE THREE

The sitting room, early morning. Ivan stands in yesterday's clothes. Zhenya enters, tired and depressed. When they do speak it's in hushed tones – Natalia is asleep on the sofa.

Ivan Do you want some tea?

Zhenya ignores Ivan. She goes to the washing machine and starts unloading it till she can take no more.

Zhenya Where were you last night?

Ivan Is that a question, or an accusation?

Zhenya This isn't a joke! Don't be an ass! (*Shouting.*) Kolya!! You're late now!

Ivan (*quiet but irritated*) Shut up.

Ivan nods at Natalia.

She's asleep.

Zhenya looks at the sleeping Natalia with disgust. Ivan exits.

(*From off.*) Kolya honey, Mama says it's time to get up.

Natalia opens her eyes furtively, then shuts them. Ivan re-enters.

Zhenya So. Where were you?

Ivan doesn't say anything, half shrugs and looks sour. Zhenya bends down and continues to talk as she unloads the washing machine. Natalia is listening.

You didn't come back, Ivan.

Zhenya continues pulling clothes out of the washing machine.

Well, you were obviously with her –
(*Shouting.*) Kolya! Get up!

Ivan shakes his head.

Ivan I was walking –

Zhenya All night?! Too scared to come home –

Ivan No . . . I was thinking –

Zhenya Thinking, thinking, oh he was thinking, very clever. (*Sour.*) Well we can all think, y'know.

Zhenya slams the washing-machine door with a slap and turns on Ivan. With an effort, she keeps her voice down.

I can't live like this, Ivan!

She exits, calling for Kolya. Petya enters as she exits.

Ivan You're up early, sweetheart.

Petya Mm, hi Pa – what's wrong with Mama?

Ivan (*shrugs, boyish*) Me.

Beat.

The bathroom door's coming off its hinges.

Petya Shall I mend it? I can do it after the doctor –

Ivan What's wrong with you?

Petya Nothing. We need to bribe him.

Ivan Oh right. I'll pay. You mend the door – and I'll pay Doctor Volkov.
Waste of the time, the army.

Ivan smiles at his son. He gives him a hug, a pat on the back.

I'm very fond of you.

Petya I know.

Ivan I'm fond of all of you.

Petya (*stilted*) And we're fond of you.

Zhenya re-enters.

Zhenya (*irritated*) Petya, fuck off. We need to talk –

Petya (*sprightly*) Yep.

He exits with his breakfast. Ivan paces.

Zhenya Am I going mad?

Ivan I hope not, that'd be really boring.

Zhenya Well that's what it feels like, Ivan.
Ivan? Ivan? Look at me.

Ivan looks at her. She is torn up.

Ivan Be patient and it'll get better. I can't just turn it on, it takes time. You can't demand affection –

Zhenya Then don't expect respect. You wear me down,

this is wearing me down . . . You make me so miserable, at least say – at least say something, but this evasion . . .

Beat.

Maybe you don't find me attractive any more but I can't carry on just suppressing – yes, speaking annoys you . . . but at least listen to me.

Ivan rolls his eyes.

I'm unhappy, Ivan! You don't touch me! Or ask me what's wrong!

Ivan I'm not fucking stupid, I can see you're unhappy.

Kolya enters in his school uniform. Ivan ruffles his son's hair.

Hello, little man.

Zhenya We're going.

Kolya But Mama –

Zhenya No, we're going.

Kolya looks longingly to the breakfast cupboard.

Kolya But what about Sugar Krinkles?

Zhenya explodes.

Zhenya I'll buy you bloody breakfast, Kolya!

Zhenya sweeps Kolya out.
Ivan steps round the sofa and looks at Natalia pretending to be asleep.

Ivan Good morning . . .
Are you pretending to be asleep?
Natalia – I can see you're awake . . .

Natalia opens her eyes.

(*Friendly.*) We have lift-off. Good morning.

Natalia swings upright and interrupts Ivan.

Natalia Who the fuck is she?!

Ivan looks puzzled, and then looks over his shoulder at the open door.

Ivan (*dumbfounded*) Who?

Natalia The woman, you met some woodpecker bitch last night.

Ivan shuts the door.

Don't lie to me, I know you met someone.
They followed you – who is she?

Ivan No one. Greta Fleishman, she's not even a friend, she happened to come in, I couldn't get rid of her – she was an accountant when I worked at the bank . . . she's a fucking boring drunk . . .
Who the fuck followed me!?

Pause.

Natalia I'm not doing this any more.

Ivan What exactly are you not doing any more?

Natalia This . . . I can't do it.
You belong to them, Ivan.

Ivan Can I make a suggestion –

Natalia No you can't. If you want to say something, say it, otherwise shut up. (*Serious.*) This isn't safe any more, Ivan. I'm not welcome . . . I've got to leave – now.

Thomas enters.

Thomas Priviet.

Natalia Hello –

Thomas Sash not up yet?

Natalia No, no. Sasha, she went to bed late. Well, you saw.

Ivan Azlip.

Ivan mimes sleeping. Tom smiles and sits down with his book. He begins to read, to their annoyance. Ivan hesitates and then speaks to Natalia.

Would you like an orange?

Tom shifts his weight, looks up and smiles innocently. They nod at him . . .

Natalia It's not safe.

Beat.

Let's go for a walk.

Ivan (*calm*) I want to eat an orange, sit down.

Thomas takes out his iPhone and plugs his headphones in.

Look, he's not even listening. Let's have an orange.

He speaks as he peels the orange.

Have you ever been to the Pushkin Museum?

Natalia No, no I haven't . . .

Ivan Oh, you should really go . . . they've got some brilliant Monets.

Natalia is lost: what is Ivan going on about?

You do know who Monet is . . .

Natalia Yes? He does water lilies.

Ivan That's right . . . the museum's got two or three of his Rouen Cathedral, have you ever seen them?

Natalia (*baffled*) I've never been to the museum, so why'd I –

Ivan When I was young I never saw the point in them. They look like ice cream melting. I mean it half looks like a cathedral.

I was standing too close, how could've I possibly seen what was going on? . . . Wasted on youth.

He looks at her intently.

Step back, everything comes into focus. For me, it seemed like falling in love, magical. Half shut your eyes, and something comes to life.

They are talking about art, but their faces tell a completely different story.

Natalia Sorry. Um, be clearer . . .

Ivan takes his time. He clarifies what he means by putting his hand on his chest whenever he says the word 'picture'. Whenever he says 'people' he motions to Natalia.

Ivan People look at pictures too quickly. People make their minds up and jump to conclusions, like our friend Greta Fleishman. Truth is, people want to get to the next one.

Don't be told what to think, make your own mind up.

Natalia That's not fair, that's / not why –

Ivan I haven't finished. I think the point of this picture is to step back, and not be *so hasty*.

He licks the orange juice off his fingers.

But I understand this is no good for you. You're young and busy – you want the next picture.

Natalia No! That's not it at all, it's, it's – it's *this*.

She carefully nods at Tom and opens her hands out – signifying the room, the situation.

Ivan Well this, I agree, *this* is no way to look at pictures.

He falls silent and touches his temple.

Natalia Ivan?

Ivan stares out to sea.

It's over. I'm sorry.

Ivan Don't be, it couldn't be helped.

Ivan hands Natalia a piece of orange.

Here.

Natalia takes it.

Natalia Thank you, darling.

Blackout.

SCENE FOUR

Sasha sits on the floor, reading. She rests her lower back against the base of the sofa. Tom sits on the sofa, looking at Sasha. He swings his body into a rather painful contortion to get closer to her. It involves resting heavily on an elbow. The sofa is too short, and his legs dangle off from mid-calf. He strokes her hair. She ignores him, and turns the page of her book.

Thomas What're you reading?

Sasha A book –

Thomas (*keen*) Cool.

Sasha looks back at Tom. She can't help but note his uncomfortable position. He grins.

Actually bloody uncomfortable.

Sasha smiles, but goes back to her book. Tom continues stroking her hair, but she moves her head away. He sits up and shakes his arm out. He looks at her balefully.

Sasha turns round and they are quick to smile at each other. When she returns to her book, the true mixed expressions on their faces come back.

Thomas Sasha, what's happened?

Beat.

I know something's happened, don't put up this cold – wall.
    I can't reach you . . . it's like my visa's run out.

Sasha It has.

Thomas I was talking metaphorically . . . it's like I'm not welcome any more.
    Sasha, look at me.

But Sasha won't look at Tom.

Thomas Don't do this – don't stop talking to me.
    It's a fluke we ever met . . .
    We're not going to bump into each other again.

Sasha is pointedly not looking at Thomas. She might cry if she sees him, but he's none the wiser. All he has is her cold hunched back.

Sasha You'll be fine.

Thomas No, I won't . . . You're kinder than this –

Sasha You don't know me well enough.

Thomas You won't let me!
    When I'm in England – I stare at the moon and wonder if it's the same for you, can you see my moon? . . . And maybe if you can . . . you could feel my love from so far away? I sit there, bouncing my love off the moon to you.

Don't forget me. Please don't forget me –
I won't ever forget you.

Sasha It's over.

Silence.

Thomas I know you cared, I cared. It wasn't a dream . . . Now you don't care any more. And I still care.

Sasha It's better this way . . .

Thomas You pride yourself on being so honest. You can't even admit you're having a relationship with the person you're having it with.

Sasha We weren't –

Thomas You wanna keep everyone in the dark. Including me.

Sasha I thought you understood the situation. I never said anything was happening.

Thomas You said it in different ways. In code – like your dad.

Sasha Don't talk about my father.

Thomas Give me my phone back then.

Petya enters and nods hello. Tom forces a smile. Sasha leaps up and embraces Petya.

Sasha (*overjoyed*) Petya, where've you been?

Petya frowns, Clara enters.

Clara Hello you.

Sasha Oh my God –

Sasha embraces Clara.

Clara You look like you've seen a ghost.

Sasha Sorry, how're you?! – You look great though.

Petya Guess who I saw today, Sasha . . . Doctor Volkov, baby –

Sasha What did he say?

Petya He wants to talk to Papa, but it's basically done. Good, huh?

Sasha What's it got to do with Papa?

Petya Cos Papa's paying.

Sasha But you can't criticise him if he's funding you. Why can't you just do it on your own?

Petya is annoyed. There is no pleasing Sasha.

Petya I thought you'd be pleased. I did it to please you. I dunno why I bother. (*Peeved.*) I thought you were going out for a meal?

Clara That's sweet, where you going?

Sasha (*shrugs*) McDonald's.

Petya (*laughing*) That's sophisticated.

Sasha He really wants to eat a Russian McDonald's.

Natalia enters with sunglasses propped on her head, dragging her heavy suitcase. Sasha turns away, pointedly.

Petya Where're you off to?

Natalia Friend's got a room free, yeah –

She looks nervous.

Clara Do you need a lift? We'll give you a lift.

Petya (*wearily*) Where are you going?

Clara We'll give her a lift, Petya –

Natalia It's fine honestly, I can manage.

Clara raises her hand to silence Natalia's excuses, and tries to take her suitcase. It's too heavy.

Clara Petya, take her suitcase.

Petya strains with Natalia's suitcase. Tom stands up to help . . .

Petya You always pack this light?

Natalia Sorry, I've got a lot of baggage.

Something sparks in Sasha's eyes.

Sasha Yes, well . . . have you said goodbye to everyone?

Natalia I think so.

Petya drags her bag and exits with Clara. Sasha is edgy.

Are we going to say goodbye?

Sasha Of course . . .

Sasha hugs Natalia. Natalia tries to pull away but Sasha has her locked in the embrace. She is whispering something in Natalia's ear. She lets go, and they part. Natalia looks shocked.

Natalia (*panicked*) But I didn't call you a bitch.

Sasha Yeah – I called *you* a bitch.

Natalia Oh, right.

Pause. Natalia is hot under the collar.

Sasha He heard everything – you were talking to Dad –

Natalia What, when?

Sasha presses play on Thomas's iPhone. [Italicised dialogue is the recorded conversation between Ivan and Natalia.]

Ivan '... *I agree,* this *is no way to look at pictures* ...'

Natalia's eyes bulge, to Sasha's satisfaction.

Natalia '*Ivan?*'

Sasha Remember this?!

Natalia '... *It's over. I'm sorry.*'

Ivan '*Don't be, it couldn't be helped.*'

Natalia We were talking about art – you can hear that / if you –

Ivan '*Here.*'

Natalia '*Thank you, darling.*'

Sasha Darling?! Darling?! You weren't talking about art so you can stop pretending –

She presses 'stop', Natalia turns on Thomas.

Natalia You saw us talking, nothing happened, did it?

Thomas Something was obviously happening ... Ah, I'm not doing this!

Natalia I'm leaving –

Sasha We gave you somewhere to live –

Natalia Yes, you did –

Sasha (*indignant*) You're smiling?!

Natalia (*scared yet helplessly beaming*) I can't help it –

Sasha What about my mum?! Stop fucking smiling –
My mother helped you – she helped you get the job.

Natalia Yeah, and I'm really, grateful –

Thomas Sasha, leave it.

Sasha You accused my father cos you knew it was the best way of hiding – no one'd suspect you if you were the one who shot him down!

She pushes Natalia, lightly.

When did it start!

Thomas holds Sasha back.

Thomas Sash, come on –

Sasha Fuck off.

Natalia Don't you dare talk to him like that!

Natalia starts to move away, towards the door.

Look, I'm sorry you made this, there's been this – whatever. I've gotta go, y'know I'm sorry –

Sasha bars Natalia's exit.

Sasha Answer the question.

Natalia doesn't speak. She just picks Sasha's hand off her shoulder.

Answer the question.

Natalia Yeah, you haven't asked a question.

Sasha I'm not going to move till you tell me the truth.

Natalia I have. Move.

Zhenya and Alexander cheerfully enter through Natalia's blocked exit.

Zhenya (*to Alexander*) See, we're not too late –

Alexander (*to Natalia*) Can't we persuade you to stay?

Natalia looks blankly at Alexander. She hasn't heard him, the blood's thick in her ears.

Zhenya But you're living very close, Natalia? The new flat's off the boulevard, no?

Natalia Sorry, yeah.

Zhenya Yeah, see. (*To Alexander.*) Her flat's off the boulevard.

Alexander (*big smile*) Very close then – what fun.

Zhenya Oh come here. You've been such a friend.

She embraces a wooden Natalia. Sasha glowers. Tom doesn't quite know where to look.

Such a support, looking after Kolya. I'm sorry it ended like this.

Alexander You understand. Our situation.

Natalia nods dully. An awkward beat.

Zhenya You'll keep in touch though.

Natalia gives a tight smile. Alexander pats Sasha's head.

Alexander Sasha's very fond of you.

Sasha (*quiet, pained*) Don't pat me.

Clara enters.

Clara Petya says the car's making a noise again?

Zhenya Tell him Ivan's taking it in tomorrow morning.

They stand for a moment. It's not quite awkward enough but nothing is being said.

Clara Shall we go then?

Natalia Great.

Alexander hugs Natalia.

Alexander Goodbye.

Zhenya Poka / Poka –

Alexander Poka –

Natalia (*as she exits*) Poka.

Tom tries to stroke Sasha's arm. She is allergic to his touch. Zhenya deals with laundry. Alexander looks at his granddaughter.

Sasha It was her! She was the other woman, she was the affair!

Zhenya Well of course it was. She's a twit –

Sasha You knew! You knew!

Zhenya Of course.

Sasha But – you said, you said all that stuff, how lovely she is . . .
Thanks for looking after Kolya, all that crap –

Zhenya There's no need to be rude.

Sasha She slept with your husband!

Zhenya answers this with a sigh. It is not unhappy. It's like she is remembering a distant summer holiday.

Zhenya Well yes . . . that's true . . . but does that really matter?

Alexander People spying on each other, betraying each other – we're old, we've lived through worse things than this.

Sasha You knew as well?!

Alexander It was an open secret. Who moves their P.A. into their flat?

Zhenya holds up a small T-shirt.

Zhenya Look, the stain came out. Kolya will be pleased.

Sasha That's Papa's T-shirt. You've shrunk it.

Beat.

Alexander Sasha, no one sizes up. Forgive them. Life is miserable without forgiveness.

Tom puts his hand out to Sasha. The lights fade.

Blackout.

SCENE FIVE

Alexander sits on the sofa. He is having a rest. He looks old and tired. Kolya is at his feet, drawing. Zhenya tidies up the room. She looks at her watch.

Zhenya Sasha will just be saying goodbye to Tom . . .

She continues tidying up.

Kolya Dyeda . . . what's the grossest thing you ever ate?

Beat. Alexander looks thoughtful.

Alexander A crow.

Kolya Have you ever eaten a cat?

Alexander . . . Plenty of cats.

Kolya Y'know when you eat cat, yeah, and afterwards when you burp, sometimes you need to burp afterwards, yeah, but does it come out like miaow?

Alexander . . . Ate a dog once.

Kolya What kind?

Alexander Alsatian – gave us indigestion.

Kolya (*pityingly*) Cos of the fur?

Alexander We ate it raw.

Kolya Like sushi?

Zhenya Leave Dedushka alone.

Alexander Ate a leather belt once too, but we boiled that. My papa had to hold his trousers up till he found some string.

Kolya Why didn't you eat like us?

Alexander It was the war. We were trapped in Leningrad. The Germans surrounded the city. We were starving. When the lake froze we escaped. There was a convoy of trucks but no petrol, so they all ran on perfume. (*To Zhenya.*) What was the name of the stuff?

Zhenya Red Moscow?

Alexander Maybe, can't remember . . . It'll come to me . . . Whatever it was called, the fumes smelled gorgeous. And then I lived here. With Anka, we had two beautiful, two boys . . .

Alexander takes out his necklace, to show Kolya.

Zhenya (*kindly*) That's enough, you'll scare him

Alexander kisses his necklace.

Kolya Why do you do that?

Zhenya Dedushka doesn't feel well.

Zhenya touches Alexander's forehead, taking his temperature.

(*To Kolya.*) Let's do something . . . do you want to go to the park?

Alexander Yes. We'll all go to the park. I'll rest, then we'll all go for a lovely walk.

Sasha enters. She has been crying. Her eyes are swollen and red.

Zhenya Sasha, oh kotik . . .

She takes her daughter in her arms.

Sasha (*disgusted*) It was horrible.

Sasha buries herself into her mother's neck. Alexander looks tentatively at Sasha, weighing up his approach.

Alexander I saw his eyes following you . . . weren't his eyes like a cat's?

Kolya instantly looks up gleefully.

Kolya Is it a story?

Zhenya Not now, Kolya.

Alexander You hypnotised him, his eyes were like a metronome.
Tick tock, tick tock, and he never stopped smiling . . . Great big smile from ear to ear.

Zhenya (*to Kolya*) Stop scribbling.

Kolya I'm bored.

Zhenya Go to your room, please. We need to have a grown-up conversation.

Kolya And then we go for a walk?

Zhenya Yes –

Sasha Just go, Kolya.

Kolya exits.

Alexander I don't think this sounds like an ending to me.

Sasha What'm I doing with my life?

Ivan enters. He sees his daughter in his wife's arms.

Ivan Your eyes are like poached eggs.
Come here, let Papa hug you.

Sasha I don't want to be hugged by you.

Ivan looks put out, rightly. Zhenya explains.

Zhenya It didn't work out with the boy.

Ivan (*shrug*) No matter. He lives in England . . .

Everyone looks at Ivan with questioning eyes.

Well, he had a fat arse.

Sasha Why can't you be nicer?

Ivan Trust me, Sasha, this is melodrama, don't blow this out of proportion. You said there wasn't anything going on anyway. Right? You said you didn't like him any more. You kept saying you wished he was gone.

He turns to present company.

Well, am I right or am I right?

Sasha (*incensed*) Why can't you be nicer, y'know, why can't you be more sympathetic –

Ivan puts his hands in his pockets and looks down. He kicks an imaginary pebble.

Why do you have to be so horrible all the time?
You can see I'm upset –

Ivan Yeah you're making a real song and dance about it!

Sasha Be sorry for me!

Ivan I think you'll find this is just hysteria.

Sasha I'm upset, Mama! And he doesn't care.

Ivan shakes his head with disbelief.

Y'know we all know, y'know, why *she* disappeared.

Ivan (*softly*) Be very careful.

He doesn't shout. He speaks judiciously.

In fact, I suggest you leave the room before you say something you truly regret.

Sasha No, I wanna do this, I wanna speak out –

Ivan Well I'm telling you, you don't, and I'm telling you to get out –

Zhenya That's enough –

Ivan speaks, while using a sweeping-away hand gesture.

Ivan (*steel*) Fuck. Off.

Sasha You screwed her! That's why she went! You fucked / her –

Ivan I will not be spied on in my own flat!!

Sasha The only reason you know that was cos *she* was spying on *us*. She was your informer –

Ivan (*hard*) Get out! Vanish! You sign up to that side, you can get out of my house!

Beat.

I mean it. Get out. You're not welcome any more. Get out!!

Sasha You want me to disappear.

And Sasha goes. A moment. Zhenya and Alexander stare at Ivan.

Zhenya Ivan – what're you doing?

Ivan I'm not having this – some foreigner, recording my conversations!

Zhenya (*quietly*) You're cross because you're guilty.

They look at each other. An impasse.

No negotiation. No communication. Cold war. You disgust me.

Zhenya exits in a rage. Ivan is left with his father. Ivan strokes his stubble. Alexander smiles and rolls a shoulder as if it's stiff. Pause.

Alexander When you were growing up we had that cat . . . Do you remember the kitten? Maybe it was before you were born . . . I was very fond of it, but we couldn't keep it . . . Zhulik, I think he was called? I suppose that's of no importance . . .
Zhulik was always ruining the furniture. Sharpening his claws on the what-have-you – and spraying everywhere, all the time.

He smiles.

Just when we thought we had everything just so, something else was ruined. In the end, we had to get rid of him . . .

Beat.

People don't forget. History shames us . . . Go down this path, where does it end? Turning on your family. Gulags and show trials. I know you, Ivan. You're my son. You're funny and tender. Much bigger than this.

Ivan looks at Alexander, willing himself not to cry.

Ivan Yeah . . . yeah . . . you look like shit. I'm going to call the doctor again.

Alexander (*grins*) It's stress, it'll go.

Beat. Alexander takes Ivan's hand.

Ivan Have you eaten anything today?

Alexander Maybe it's blood sugar, give me a sweet.

Ivan hands him a sweet. Alexander's hands are shaking. He cannot unwrap the sweet.

Ivan I'll unwrap it.

Ivan takes the sweet and unwraps it.

Alexander I'm fine, you're fussing.

Ivan hands Alexander the sweet and looks at him again.

Ivan I think I'll call the doctor anyway.

Alexander tries to speak with the sweet in his mouth. He rolls it to one cheek. His voice is punctuated with slurping back the excess spit.

Alexander Told you – blood sugar – don't fuss.

Ivan walks to the door.

Ivan.

Ivan stands at the door and looks back at his father.

Ivan What, Pa?

Alexander I love you, that's why this hurts.

Alexander touches his heart. Ivan nods and exits. A moment passes then Alexander looks worried. He tries to speak but nothing comes. He thinks he's choking on the sweet, so he spits it out. He looks at the boiled sweet in his hand. It terrifies him like it's pure evil. He tries to stand up but something holds him down. He's having a heart attack. He rolls over, heaving for a moment and settles. Kolya enters.

Kolya Dyedu? What're you doing? We're all waiting for you.

Alexander doesn't respond.

(*Uncertainly.*) Mama says . . . she says napping wastes the day.

Beat.

Alexander Who is it?

Kolya Kolya.

Alexander rolls over and sees his Kolya. He is heartbroken.

Alexander Nikolai . . . You came back.

Alexander takes Kolya in properly.

(*Shocked.*) Your eyes are so big, what did they do to you?

With a shaky hand, Alexander holds out the sweet covered in spittle.

Here – eat. You must be starving.

Kolya We're all waiting for you.

Alexander Wait for me . . . I'll walk with you.

Kolya nods. Alexander slowly crosses Kolya's forehead.

Good boy.

Kolya takes Alexander's glasses off and puts them in their case.
Alexander smiles with such enduring patience.

It's alright, I want to come . . .
I told them this was my last winter.

Silence. Kolya snaps the case shut.

Blackout.

The End.